Harvard
Business
Review

ON

THE PERSUASIVE LEADER

THE HARVARD BUSINESS REVIEW PAPERBACK SERIES

The series is designed to bring today's managers and professionals the fundamental information they need to stay competitive in a fast-moving world. From the preeminent thinkers whose work has defined an entire field to the rising stars who will redefine the way we think about business, here are the leading minds and landmark ideas that have established the *Harvard Business Review* as required reading for ambitious businesspeople in organizations around the globe.

Other books in the series:

Other books in the series (continued):

Harvard Business Review

ON

THE PERSUASIVE LEADER

A HARVARD BUSINESS REVIEW PAPERBACK

The *Harvard Business Review* articles in this collection are available as
individual reprints. Discounts apply to quantity purchases. For information and ordering, please contact Customer Service, Harvard Business
School Publishing, Boston, MA 02163. Telephone: (617) 783-7500 or
(800) 988-0886, 8 A.M. to 6 P.M. Eastern Time, Monday through Friday.
Fax: (617) 783-7555, 24 hours a day. E-mail: custserv@hbsp.harvard.edu.

Library of Congress Cataloging-in-Publication Data
Harvard business review on the persuasive leader.
        p.   cm. — (A Harvard business review paperback)
    Includes index.
    ISBN-13: 978-1-4221-2499-4
    1. Leadership—Psychological aspects.   2. Persuasion (Psychology).
3. Employee motivation.   4. Decision making.   5. Organizational
change.   I. Harvard business review.   II. Title: Persuasive leader.
HD57.7.H387355   2008
658.4´092—dc22   2008003053

Contents

Harvard Business Review

ON

THE PERSUASIVE LEADER

The Necessary Art of Persuasion

JAY A. CONGER

Executive Summary

BUSINESS TODAY IS LARGELY RUN by teams and populated by authority-averse baby boomers and Generation Xers. That makes persuasion more important than ever as a managerial tool.

But contrary to popular belief, the author asserts, persuasion is not the same as selling an idea or convincing opponents to see things your way. It is instead a process of learning from others and negotiating a shared solution. To that end, persuasion consists of four essential elements: establishing credibility, framing to find common ground, providing vivid evidence, and connecting emotionally.

Credibility grows, the author says, out of two sources: expertise and relationships. The former is a function of product or process knowledge and the latter a history of listening to and working in the best interest of others.

But even if a persuader's credibility is high, his position must make sense—even more, it must appeal—to the audience. Therefore, a persuader must frame his position to illuminate its benefits to everyone who will feel its impact.

Persuasion then becomes a matter of presenting evidence—but not just ordinary charts and spreadsheets. The author says the most effective persuaders use vivid—even over-the-top—stories, metaphors, and examples to make their positions come alive.

Finally, good persuaders have the ability to accurately sense and respond to their audience's emotional state. Sometimes, that means they have to suppress their own emotions; at other times, they must intensify them.

Persuasion can be a force for enormous good in an organization, but people must understand it for what it is: an often painstaking process that requires insight, planning, and compromise.

If THERE EVER WAS A TIME for businesspeople to learn the fine art of persuasion, it is now. Gone are the command-and-control days of executives managing by decree. Today businesses are run largely by cross-functional teams of peers and populated by baby boomers and their Generation X offspring, who show little tolerance for unquestioned authority. Electronic communication and globalization have further eroded the traditional hierarchy, as ideas and people flow more freely than ever around organizations and as decisions get made closer to the markets. These fundamental changes, more than a decade in the making but now firmly part of the economic landscape, essentially come down to this: work today gets done in an environment where people don't just ask What should I do? but Why should I do it?

To answer this why question effectively is to persuade. Yet many businesspeople misunderstand persuasion, and more still underutilize it. The reason? Persuasion is widely perceived as a skill reserved for selling products and closing deals. It is also commonly seen as just another form of manipulation—devious and to be avoided. Certainly, persuasion can be used in selling and deal-clinching situations, and it can be misused to manipulate people. But exercised constructively and to its full potential, persuasion supersedes sales and is quite the opposite of deception. Effective persuasion becomes a negotiating and learning process through which a persuader leads colleagues to a problem's shared solution. Persuasion does indeed involve moving people to a position they don't currently hold, but not by begging or cajoling. Instead, it involves careful preparation, the proper framing of arguments, the presentation of vivid supporting evidence, and the effort to find the correct emotional match with your audience.

Effective persuasion is a difficult and time-consuming proposition, but it may also be more powerful than the command-and-control managerial model it succeeds. As AlliedSignal's CEO Lawrence Bossidy said recently, "The day when you could yell and scream and beat people into good performance is over. Today you have to appeal to them by helping them see how they can get from here to there, by establishing some credibility, and by giving them some reason and help to get there. Do all those things, and they'll knock down doors." In essence, he is describing persuasion—now more than ever, the language of business leadership.

Think for a moment of your definition of persuasion. If you are like most businesspeople I have encountered (see the insert "Twelve Years of Watching and Listening" at the end of this article), you see persuasion as a relatively straightforward process. First, you strongly state your position. Second, you outline the supporting arguments, followed by a highly assertive, data-based exposition. Finally, you enter the deal-making stage and work toward a "close." In other words, you use logic, persistence, and personal enthusiasm to get others to buy a good idea. The reality is that following this process is one surefire way to fail at persuasion. (See the insert "Four Ways Not to Persuade" at the end of this article.)

What, then, constitutes effective persuasion? If persuasion is a learning and negotiating process, then in the most general terms it involves phases of discovery, preparation, and dialogue. Getting ready to persuade colleagues can take weeks or months of planning as you learn about your audience and the position you intend to argue. Before they even start to talk, effective persuaders have considered their positions from every angle. What investments in time and money will my position require from others? Is my supporting evidence weak in any way? Are there alternative positions I need to examine?

Dialogue happens before and during the persuasion process. Before the process begins, effective persuaders use dialogue to learn more about their audience's opinions, concerns, and perspectives. During the process, dialogue continues to be a form of learning, but it is also the beginning of the negotiation stage. You invite people to discuss, even debate, the merits of your position, and then to offer honest feedback and suggest alternative solutions. That may sound like a slow way to achieve your goal, but effective persuasion is about testing and revising ideas in concert with your colleagues' concerns and needs. In fact, the best persuaders not only listen to others but also incorporate their perspectives into a shared solution.

Persuasion, in other words, often involves—indeed, demands—compromise. Perhaps that is why the most effective persuaders seem to share a common trait: they are open-minded, never dogmatic. They enter the persuasion process prepared to adjust their viewpoints and incorporate others' ideas. That approach to persuasion is, interestingly, highly persuasive in itself. When colleagues see that a persuader is eager to hear their views and willing to make changes in response to their needs and concerns, they respond very positively. They trust the persuader more and listen more attentively. They don't fear being bowled over or manipulated. They see the persuader as flexible and are thus more willing to make sacrifices themselves. Because that is such a powerful dynamic, good persuaders often enter the persuasion process with judicious compromises already prepared.

Four Essential Steps

Effective persuasion involves four distinct and essential steps. First, effective persuaders establish credibility. Second, they frame their goals in a way that identifies common ground with those they intend to persuade. Third, they reinforce their positions using vivid language and compelling evidence. And fourth, they connect emotionally with their audience. As one of the most effective executives in our research commented, "The most valuable lesson I've learned about persuasion over the years is that there's just as much strategy in how you present your position as in the position itself. In fact, I'd say the strategy of presentation is the more critical."

ESTABLISH CREDIBILITY

The first hurdle persuaders must overcome is their own credibility. A persuader can't advocate a new or contrarian position without having people wonder, Can we trust this individual's perspectives and opinions? Such a reaction is understandable. After all, allowing oneself to be persuaded is risky, because any new initiative demands a commitment of time and resources. Yet even though persuaders must have high credibility, our research strongly suggests that most managers overestimate their own credibility—considerably.

In the workplace, credibility grows out of two sources: expertise and relationships. People are considered to have high levels of expertise if they have a history of sound judgment or have proven themselves knowledgeable and well informed about their proposals. For example, in proposing a new product idea, an effective persuader would need to be perceived as possessing a thorough understanding of the product—its specifications, target markets, customers, and competing products. A history of prior successes would further strengthen the persuader's perceived expertise. One extremely successful executive in our research had a track record of 14 years of devising highly effective advertising campaigns. Not surprisingly, he had an easy time winning colleagues over to his position. Another manager had a track record of seven successful new-product launches in a period of five years. He, too, had an advantage when it came to persuading his colleagues to support his next new idea.

On the relationship side, people with high credibility have demonstrated—again, usually over time—that they can be trusted to listen and to work in the best interests of others. They have also consistently shown strong emotional character and integrity; that is, they are not known for mood extremes or inconsistent performance. Indeed, people who are known to be honest, steady, and reliable have an edge when going into any persuasion situation. Because their relationships are robust, they are more apt to be given the benefit of the doubt. One effective persuader in our research was considered by colleagues to be remarkably trustworthy and fair; many people confided in her. In addition, she generously shared credit for good ideas and provided staff with exposure to the company's senior executives. This woman had built strong relationships, which meant her staff and peers were always willing to consider seriously what she proposed.

If expertise and relationships determine credibility, it is crucial that you undertake an honest assessment of where you stand on both criteria before beginning to persuade. To do so, first step back and ask yourself the following questions related to expertise: How will others perceive my knowledge about the strategy, product, or change I am proposing? Do I have a track record in this area that others know about and respect? Then, to assess the strength of your relationship credibility, ask yourself, Do those I am hoping to persuade see me as helpful, trustworthy, and supportive? Will they see me as someone in sync with them—emotionally, intellectually, and politically—on issues like this one? Finally, it is important to note that it is not enough to get your own read on these matters. You must also test your answers with colleagues you trust to give you a reality check. Only then will you have a complete picture of your credibility.

In most cases, that exercise helps people discover that they have some measure of weakness, either on the expertise or on the relationship side of credibility. The challenge then becomes to fill in such gaps.

In general, if your area of weakness is on the expertise side, you have several options:

- First, you can learn more about the complexities of your position through either formal or informal education and through conversations with knowledgeable individuals. You might also get more relevant experience on the job by asking, for instance, to be assigned to a team that would increase your insight into particular markets or products.

- Another alternative is to hire someone to bolster your expertise—for example, an industry consultant or a recognized outside expert, such as a professor. Either one may have the knowledge and experience required to support your position effectively. Similarly, you may tap experts within your organization to advocate your position. Their credibility becomes a substitute for your own.

- You can also utilize other outside sources of information to support your position, such as respected business or trade periodicals, books, independently produced reports, and lectures by experts. In our research, one executive from the clothing industry successfully persuaded his company to reposition an entire product line to a more youthful market after bolstering his credibility with articles by a noted demographer in two highly regarded journals and with two independent market-research studies.

- Finally, you may launch pilot projects to demonstrate on a small scale your expertise and the value of your ideas.

As for filling in the relationship gap:

- You should make a concerted effort to meet one-on-one with all the key people you plan to persuade. This is not the time to outline your position but rather to get a range of perspectives on the issue at hand. If you have the time and resources, you should even offer to help these people with issues that concern them.

- Another option is to involve like-minded coworkers who already have strong relationships with your audience. Again, that is a matter of seeking out substitutes on your own behalf.

For an example of how these strategies can be put to work, consider the case of a chief operating officer of a large retail bank, whom we will call Tom Smith. Although he was new to his job, Smith ardently wanted to persuade the senior management team that the company was in serious trouble. He believed that the bank's overhead was excessive and would jeopardize its position as the industry entered a more competitive era. Most of his colleagues, however, did not see the potential seriousness of the situation. Because the bank had been enormously successful in recent years, they believed changes in the industry posed little danger. In addition to being newly appointed, Smith had another problem: his career had been in financial services, and he was considered an outsider in the world of retail banking. Thus he had few personal connections to draw on as he made his case, nor was he perceived to be particularly knowledgeable about marketplace exigencies.

As a first step in establishing credibility, Smith hired an external consultant with respected credentials in the industry who showed that the bank was indeed poorly positioned to be a low-cost producer. In a series of inter-active presentations to the bank's top-level management, the consultant revealed how the company's leading com-petitors were taking aggressive actions to contain oper-ating costs. He made it clear from these presentations that not cutting costs would soon cause the bank to fall drastically behind the competition. These findings were then distributed in written reports that circulated throughout the bank.

Next, Smith determined that the bank's branch man-agers were critical to his campaign. The buy-in of those respected and informed individuals would signal to others in the company that his concerns were valid. Moreover, Smith looked to the branch managers because he believed that they could increase his expertise about marketplace trends and also help him test his own assumptions. Thus, for the next three months, he visited every branch in his region of Ontario, Canada—135 in all. During each visit, he spent time with branch managers, listening to their perceptions of the bank's strengths and weaknesses. He learned firsthand about the competi-tion's initiatives and customer trends, and he solicited ideas for improving the bank's services and minimizing costs. By the time he was through, Smith had a broad perspective on the bank's future that few people even in senior management possessed. And he had built dozens of relationships in the process.

Finally, Smith launched some small but highly visible initiatives to demonstrate his expertise and capabilities.

For example, he was concerned about slow growth in the company's mortgage business and the loan officers' resulting slip in morale. So he devised a program in which new mortgage customers would make no payments for the first 90 days. The initiative proved remarkably successful, and in short order Smith appeared to be a far more savvy retail banker than anyone had assumed.

Another example of how to establish credibility comes from Microsoft. In 1990, two product-development managers, Karen Fries and Barry Linnett, came to believe that the market would greatly welcome software that featured a "social interface." They envisioned a package that would employ animated human and animal characters to show users how to go about their computing tasks.

Inside Microsoft, however, employees had immediate concerns about the concept. Software programmers ridiculed the cute characters. Animated characters had been used before only in software for children, making their use in adult environments hard to envision. But Fries and Linnett felt their proposed product had both dynamism and complexity, and they remained convinced that consumers would eagerly buy such programs. They also believed that the home-computer software market—largely untapped at the time and with fewer software standards—would be open to such innovation.

Within the company, Fries had gained quite a bit of relationship credibility. She had started out as a recruiter for the company in 1987 and had worked directly for many of Microsoft's senior executives. They trusted and liked her. In addition, she had been responsible for hiring the company's product and program managers. As a result, she knew all the senior people at Microsoft and had hired many of the people who would be deciding on her product.

Linnett's strength laid in his expertise. In particular, he knew the technology behind an innovative tutorial program called PC Works. In addition, both Fries and Linnett had managed Publisher, a product with a unique help feature called Wizards, which Microsoft's CEO, Bill Gates, had liked. But those factors were sufficient only to get an initial hearing from Microsoft's senior management. To persuade the organization to move forward, the pair would need to improve perceptions of their expertise. It hurt them that this type of social-interface software had no proven track record of success and that they were both novices with such software. Their challenge became one of finding substitutes for their own expertise.

Their first step was a wise one. From within Microsoft, they hired respected technical guru Darrin Massena. With Massena, they developed a set of prototypes to demonstrate that they did indeed understand the software's technology and could make it work. They then tested the prototypes in market research, and users responded enthusiastically. Finally, and most important, they enlisted two Stanford University professors, Clifford Nass and Bryon Reeves, both experts in human-computer interaction. In several meetings with Microsoft senior managers and Gates himself, they presented a rigorously compiled and thorough body of research that demonstrated how and why social-interface software was ideally suited to the average computer user. In addition, Fries and Linnett asserted that considerable jumps in computing power would make more realistic cartoon characters an increasingly malleable technology. Their product, they said, was the leading edge of an incipient software revolution. Convinced, Gates approved a full product-development team, and in January 1995, the product called BOB was launched. BOB went on to sell more than half a million copies, and its concept and technology are being used within Microsoft as a platform for developing several Internet products.

Credibility is the cornerstone of effective persuading; without it, a persuader won't be given the time of day. In the best-case scenario, people enter into a persuasion situation with some measure of expertise and relationship credibility. But it is important to note that credibility along either lines can be built or bought. Indeed, it must be, or the next steps are an exercise in futility.

FRAME FOR COMMON GROUND

Even if your credibility is high, your position must still appeal strongly to the people you are trying to persuade. After all, few people will jump on board a train that will bring them to ruin or even mild discomfort. Effective persuaders must be adept at describing their positions in terms that illuminate their advantages. As any parent can tell you, the fastest way to get a child to come along willingly on a trip to the grocery store is to point out that there are lollipops by the cash register. That is not deception. It is just a persuasive way of framing the benefits of taking such a journey. In work situations, persuasive framing is obviously more complex, but the underlying principle is the same. It is a process of identifying shared benefits.

Monica Ruffo, an account executive for an advertising agency, offers a good example of persuasive framing. Her client, a fast-food chain, was instituting a promotional campaign in Canada; menu items such as a hamburger, fries, and cola were to be bundled together and sold at a low price. The strategy made sense to corporate headquarters. Its research showed that consumers thought the company's products were higher priced than the competition's, and the company was anxious to overcome this perception. The franchisees, on the other hand, were still experiencing strong sales and were far more concerned about the short-term impact that the new, low prices would have on their profit margins.

A less experienced persuader would have attempted to rationalize headquarters' perspective to the franchisees—to convince them of its validity. But Ruffo framed the change in pricing to demonstrate its benefits to the franchisees themselves. The new value campaign, she explained, would actually improve franchisees' profits. To back up this point, she drew on several sources. A pilot project in Tennessee, for instance, had demonstrated that under the new pricing scheme, the sales of french fries and drinks—the two most profitable items on the menu—had markedly increased. In addition, the company had rolled out medium-sized meal packages in 80% of its U.S. outlets, and franchisees' sales of fries and drinks had jumped 26%. Citing research from a respected business periodical, Ruffo also showed that when customers raised their estimate of the value they receive from a retail establishment by 10%, the establishment's sales rose by 1%. She had estimated that the new meal plan would increase value perceptions by 100%, with the result that franchisee sales could be expected to grow 10%.

Ruffo closed her presentation with a letter written many years before by the company's founder to the organization. It was an emotional letter extolling the values of the company and stressing the importance of the franchisees to the company's success. It also highlighted the importance of the company's position as the low-price leader in the industry. The beliefs and values contained in the letter had long been etched in the minds of Ruffo's audience. Hearing them again only confirmed the company's concern for the franchisees and the importance of their winning formula. They also won Ruffo a standing ovation. That day, the franchisees voted unanimously to support the new meal-pricing plan.

The Ruffo case illustrates why—in choosing appropriate positioning—it is critical first to identify your objective's tangible benefits to the people you are trying to persuade. Sometimes that is easy. Mutual benefits exist. In other situations, however, no shared advantages are readily apparent—or meaningful. In these cases, effective persuaders adjust their positions. They know it is impossible to engage people and gain commitment to ideas or plans without highlighting the advantages to all the parties involved.

At the heart of framing is a solid understanding of your audience. Even before starting to persuade, the best persuaders we have encountered closely study the issues that matter to their colleagues. They use conversations, meetings, and other forms of dialogue to collect essential information. They are good at listening. They test their ideas with trusted confidants, and they ask questions of the people they will later be persuading. Those steps help them think through the arguments, the evidence, and the perspectives they will present. Oftentimes, this process causes them to alter or compromise their own plans before they even start persuading. It is through this thoughtful, inquisitive approach they develop frames that appeal to their audience.

Consider the case of a manager who was in charge of process engineering for a jet engine manufacturer. He had redesigned the work flow for routine turbine maintenance for airline clients in a manner that would dramatically shorten the turnaround time for servicing. Before presenting his ideas to the company's president, he consulted a good friend in the company, the vice president of engineering, who knew the president well. This conversation revealed that the president's prime concern would not be speed or efficiency but profitability. To get the president's buy-in, the vice president explained, the new system would have to improve the company's profitability in the short run by lowering operating expenses.

At first this information had the manager stumped. He had planned to focus on efficiency and had even intended to request additional funding to make the process work. But his conversation with the vice president sparked him to change his position. Indeed, he went so far as to change the work-flow design itself so that it no longer required new investment but rather drove down costs. He then carefully documented the cost savings and profitability gains that his new plan would produce and presented this revised plan to the president. With his initiative positioned anew, the manager persuaded the president and got the project approved.

PROVIDE EVIDENCE

With credibility established and a common frame identified, persuasion becomes a matter of presenting evidence. Ordinary evidence, however, won't do. We have found that the most effective persuaders use language in a particular way. They supplement numerical data with examples, stories, metaphors, and analogies to make their positions come alive. That use of language paints a vivid word picture and, in doing so, lends a compelling and tangible quality to the persuader's point of view.

Think about a typical persuasion situation. The persuader is often advocating a goal, strategy, or initiative with an uncertain outcome. Karen Fries and Barry Linnett, for instance, wanted Microsoft to invest millions of dollars in a software package with chancy technology and unknown market demand. The team could have supported its case solely with market research, financial projections, and the like. But that would have been a mistake, because research shows that most people perceive such reports as not entirely informative. They are too abstract to be completely meaningful or memorable. In essence, the numbers don't make an emotional impact.

By contrast, stories and vivid language do, particularly when they present comparable situations to the one under discussion. A marketing manager trying to persuade senior executives to invest in a new product, for example, might cite examples of similar investments that paid off handsomely. Indeed, we found that people readily draw lessons from such cases. More important, the research shows that listeners absorb information in proportion to its vividness. Thus it is no wonder that Fries and Linnett hit a home run when they presented their case for BOB with the following analogy:

> *Imagine you want to cook dinner and you must first go to the supermarket. You have all the flexibility you want— you can cook anything in the world as long as you know how and have the time and desire to do it. When you arrive at the supermarket, you find all these overstuffed aisles with cryptic single-word headings like "sundries" and "ethnic food" and "condiments." These are the menus on typical computer interfaces. The question is whether salt is under condiments or ethnic food or near the potato*

chip section. There are surrounding racks and wall spaces, much as our software interfaces now have support buttons, tool bars, and lines around the perimeters. Now after you have collected everything, you still need to put it all together in the correct order to make a meal. If you're a good cook, your meal will probably be good. If you're a novice, it probably won't be.

We [at Microsoft] have been selling under the supermarket category for years, and we think there is a big opportunity for restaurants. That's what we are trying to do now with BOB: pushing the next step with software that is more like going to a restaurant, so the user doesn't spend all of his time searching for the ingredients. We find and put the ingredients together. You sit down, you get comfortable. We bring you a menu. We do the work, you relax. It's an enjoyable experience. No walking around lost trying to find things, no cooking.

Had Fries and Linnett used a literal description of BOB's advantages, few of their highly computer-literate colleagues at Microsoft would have personally related to the menu-searching frustration that BOB was designed to eliminate. The analogy they selected, however, made BOB's purpose both concrete and memorable.

A master persuader, Mary Kay Ash, the founder of Mary Kay Cosmetics, regularly draws on analogies to illustrate and "sell" the business conduct she values. Consider this speech at the company's annual sales convention:

Back in the days of the Roman Empire, the legions of the emperor conquered the known world. There was, however, one band of people that the Romans never conquered. Those people were the followers of the great teacher from Bethlehem. Historians have long since discovered that one of the reasons for the sturdiness of this folk was their habit of meeting together weekly. They shared their difficulties, and they stood side by side. Does this remind you of something? The way we stand side by side and share our knowledge and difficulties with each other in our weekly unit meetings? I have so often observed when a director or unit member is confronted with a personal problem that the unit stands together in helping that sister in distress. What a wonderful circle of friendships we have. Perhaps it's one of the greatest fringe benefits of our company.

Through her vivid analogy, Ash links collective support in the company to a courageous period in Christian history. In doing so, she accomplishes several objectives. First, she drives home her belief that collective support is crucial to the success of the organization. Most Mary Kay salespeople are independent operators who face the daily challenges of direct selling. An emotional support system of fellow salespeople is essential to ensure that self-esteem and confidence remain intact in the face of rejection. Next she suggests by her analogy that solidarity against the odds is the best way to stymie powerful oppressors—to wit, the competition. Finally, Ash's choice of analogy imbues a sense of a heroic mission to the work of her sales force.

You probably don't need to invoke the analogy of the Christian struggle to support your position, but effective persuaders are not afraid of unleashing the immense power of language. In fact, they use it to their utmost advantage.

CONNECT EMOTIONALLY

In the business world, we like to think that our colleagues use reason to make their decisions, yet if we scratch below the surface we will always find emotions at play. Good persuaders are aware of the primacy of emotions and are responsive to them in two important ways. First, they show their own emotional commitment to the position they are advocating. Such expression is a delicate matter. If you act too emotional, people may doubt your clearheadedness. But you must also show that your commitment to a goal is not just in your mind but in your heart and gut as well. Without this demonstration of feeling, people may wonder if you actually believe in the position you're championing.

Perhaps more important, however, is that effective persuaders have a strong and accurate sense of their audience's emotional state, and they adjust the tone of their arguments accordingly. Sometimes that means coming on strong, with forceful points. Other times, a whisper may be all that is required. The idea is that whatever your position, you match your emotional fervor to your audience's ability to receive the message.

Effective persuaders seem to have a second sense about how their colleagues have interpreted past events in the organization and how they will probably interpret a proposal. The best persuaders in our study would usually canvass key individuals who had a good pulse on the mood and emotional expectations of those about to be persuaded. They would ask those individuals how various proposals might affect colleagues on an emotional level—in essence, testing possible reactions. They were also quite effective at gathering information through informal conversations in the hallways or at lunch. In the end, their aim was to ensure that the emotional appeal behind their persuasion matched what their audience was already feeling or expecting.

To illustrate the importance of emotional match-making in persuasion, consider this example. The president of an aeronautics manufacturing company strongly believed that the maintenance costs and turnaround time of the company's U.S. and foreign competitors were so much better than his own company's that it stood to lose customers and profits. He wanted to communicate his fear and his urgent desire for change to his senior managers. So one afternoon, he called them into the boardroom. On an overhead screen was the projected image of a smiling man flying an old-fashioned biplane with his scarf blowing in the wind. The right half of the transparency was covered. When everyone was seated, the president explained that he felt as this pilot did, given the company's recent good fortune. The organization, after all, had just finished its most successful year in history. But then with a deep sigh, he announced that his happiness was quickly vanishing. As the president lifted the remaining portion of the sheet, he revealed an image of the pilot flying directly into a wall. The president then faced his audience and in a heavy voice said, "This is what I see happening to us." He asserted that the company was headed for a crash if people didn't take action fast. He then went on to lecture the group about the steps needed to counter this threat.

The reaction from the group was immediate and negative. Directly after the meeting, managers gathered in small clusters in the hallways to talk about the president's "scare tactics." They resented what they perceived to be the president's overstatement of the case. As the managers saw it, they had exerted enormous effort that year to break the company's records in sales and profitability. They were proud of their achievements. In fact, they had entered the meeting expecting it would be the moment of recognition. But to their absolute surprise, they were scolded.

The president's mistake? First, he should have canvassed a few members of his senior team to ascertain the emotional state of the group. From that, he would have learned that they were in need of thanks and recognition. He should then have held a separate session devoted simply to praising the team's accomplishments. Later, in a second meeting, he could have expressed his own anxieties about the coming year. And rather than blame the team for ignoring the future, he could have calmly described what he saw as emerging threats to the company and then asked his management team to help him develop new initiatives.

Now let us look at someone who found the right emotional match with his audience: Robert Marcell, head of Chrysler's small-car design team. In the early 1990s, Chrysler was eager to produce a new subcompact—indeed, the company had not introduced a new model of this type since 1978. But senior managers at Chrysler did not want to go it alone. They thought an alliance with a foreign manufacturer would improve the car's design and protect Chrysler's cash stores.

Marcell was convinced otherwise. He believed that the company should bring the design and production of a new subcompact in-house. He knew that persuading senior managers would be difficult, but he also had his own team to contend with. Team members had lost their confidence that they would ever again have the opportunity to create a good car. They were also angry that the United States had once again given up its position to foreign competitors when it came to small cars.

Marcell decided that his persuasion tactics had to be built around emotional themes that would touch his audience. From innumerable conversations around the company, he learned that many people felt as he did—

that to surrender the subcompact's design to a foreign manufacturer was to surrender the company's soul and, ultimately, its ability to provide jobs. In addition, he felt deeply that his organization was a talented group hungry for a challenge and an opportunity to restore its self-esteem and pride. He would need to demonstrate his faith in the team's abilities.

Marcell prepared a 15-minute talk built around slides of his hometown, Iron River, a now defunct mining town in Upper Michigan, devastated, in large part, by foreign mining companies. On the screen flashed recent photographs he had taken of his boarded-up high school, the shuttered homes of his childhood friends, the crumbling ruins of the town's ironworks, closed churches, and an abandoned railroad yard. After a description of each of these places, he said the phrase, "We couldn't compete"—like the refrain of a hymn. Marcell's point was that the same outcome awaited Detroit if the production of small cars was not brought back to the United States. Surrender was the enemy, he said, and devastation would follow if the group did not take immediate action.

Marcell ended his slide show on a hopeful note. He spoke of his pride in his design group and then challenged the team to build a "made-in-America" subcompact that would prove that the United States could still compete. The speech, which echoed the exact sentiments of the audience, rekindled the group's fighting spirit. Shortly after the speech, group members began drafting their ideas for a new car.

Marcell then took his slide show to the company's senior management and ultimately to Chrysler chairman Lee Iacocca. As Marcell showed his slides, he could see that Iacocca was touched. Iacocca, after all, was a fighter and a strongly patriotic man himself. In fact, Marcell's approach was not too different from Iacocca's earlier appeal to the United States Congress to save Chrysler. At the end of the show, Marcell stopped and said, "If we dare to be different, we could be the reason the U.S. auto industry survives. We could be the reason our kids and grandkids don't end up working at fast-food chains." Iacocca stayed on for two hours as Marcell explained in greater detail what his team was planning. Afterward, Iacocca changed his mind and gave Marcell's group approval to develop a car, the Neon.

With both groups, Marcell skillfully matched his emotional tenor to that of the group he was addressing. The ideas he conveyed resonated deeply with his largely Midwestern audience. And rather than leave them in a depressed state, he offered them hope, which was more persuasive than promising doom. Again, this played to the strong patriotic sentiments of his American-heartland audience.

No effort to persuade can succeed without emotion, but showing too much emotion can be as unproductive as showing too little. The important point to remember is that you must match your emotions to your audience's.

The Force of Persuasion

The concept of persuasion, like that of power, often confuses and even mystifies businesspeople. It is so complex—and so dangerous when mishandled—that many would rather just avoid it altogether. But like power, persuasion can be a force for enormous good in an organization. It can pull people together, move ideas forward, galvanize change, and forge constructive solutions. To do all that, however, people must understand persuasion for what it is—not convincing and selling but learning and negotiating. Furthermore, it must be seen as an art form that requires commitment and practice, especially as today's business contingencies make persuasion more necessary than ever.

Twelve Years of Watching and Listening

THE IDEAS BEHIND THIS ARTICLE spring from three streams of research.

For the last 12 years as both an academic and as a consultant, I have been studying 23 senior business leaders who have shown themselves to be effective change agents. Specifically, I have investigated how these individuals use language to motivate their employees, articulate vision and strategy, and mobilize their organizations to adapt to challenging business environments.

Four years ago, I started a second stream of research exploring the capabilities and characteristics of successful cross-functional team leaders. The core of my database comprised interviews with and observations of 18 individuals working in a range of U.S. and Canadian companies. These were not senior leaders as in my earlier studies but low- and middle-level managers. Along with interviewing the colleagues of these people, I also compared their skills with those of other team leaders—in particular, with the leaders of less successful cross-functional teams engaged in similar initiatives within the same companies. Again, my focus was on language, but I also studied the influence of interpersonal skills.

The similarities in the persuasion skills possessed by both the change-agent leaders and effective team leaders prompted me to explore the academic literature on persuasion and rhetoric, as well as on the art of gospel preaching. Meanwhile, to learn how most managers approach the persuasion process, I observed several dozen managers in company meetings, and I employed simulations in company executive-education programs where groups of managers had to persuade one another on hypothetical business objectives. Finally, I selected a group of 14 managers known for their outstanding abilities in constructive persuasion. For several months, I interviewed them and their colleagues and observed them in actual work situations.

Four Ways Not to Persuade

IN MY WORK WITH MANAGERS as a researcher and as a consultant, I have had the unfortunate opportunity to see executives fail miserably at persuasion. Here are the four most common mistakes people make:

1. **They attempt to make their case with an up-front, hard sell.** I call this the John Wayne approach. Managers strongly state their position at the outset, and then through a process of persistence, logic, and exuberance, they try to push the idea to a close. In reality, setting out a strong position at the start of a persuasion effort gives potential opponents something to grab onto—and fight against. It's far better to present your position with the finesse and reserve of a lion tamer, who engages his "partner" by showing him the legs of a chair. In other words, effective persuaders don't begin the process by giving their colleagues a clear target in which to set their jaws.

2. **They resist compromise.** Too many managers see compromise as surrender, but it is essential to constructive persuasion. Before people buy into a proposal, they

want to see that the persuader is flexible enough to respond to their concerns. Compromises can often lead to better, more sustainable shared solutions.

By not compromising, ineffective persuaders unconsciously send the message that they think persuasion is a one-way street. But persuasion is a process of give-and-take. Kathleen Reardon, a professor of organizational behavior at the University of Southern California, points out that a persuader rarely changes another person's behavior or viewpoint without altering his or her own in the process. To persuade meaningfully, we must not only listen to others but also incorporate their perspectives into our own.

3. **They think the secret of persuasion lies in presenting great arguments.** In persuading people to change their minds, great arguments matter. No doubt about it. But arguments, per se, are only one part of the equation. Other factors matter just as much, such as the persuader's credibility and his or her ability to create a proper, mutually beneficial frame for a position, connect on the right emotional level with an audience, and communicate through vivid language that makes arguments come alive.

4. **They assume persuasion is a one-shot effort.** Persuasion is a process, not an event. Rarely, if ever, is it possible to arrive at a shared solution on the first try. More often than not, persuasion involves listening to people, testing a position, developing a new position that reflects input from the group, more testing, incorporating compromises, and then trying again. If this sounds like a slow and difficult process, that's because it is. But the results are worth the effort.

Originally published in May–June 1998
Reprint 98304

Harnessing the Science of Persuasion

ROBERT B. CIALDINI

Executive Summary

IF LEADERSHIP, AT ITS MOST BASIC, consists of getting things done through others, then persuasion is one of the leader's essential tools. Many executives have assumed that this tool is beyond their grasp, available only to the charismatic and the eloquent. Over the past several decades, though, experimental psychologists have learned which methods reliably lead people to concede, comply, or change. Their research shows that persuasion is governed by several principles that can be taught and applied.

The first principle is that people are more likely to follow someone who is similar to them than someone who is not. Wise managers, then, enlist peers to help make their cases. Second, people are more willing to cooperate with those who are not only like them but who like them, as well. So it's worth the time to uncover real similarities and offer genuine praise.

Third, experiments confirm the intuitive truth that people tend to treat you the way you treat them. It's sound policy to do a favor before seeking one. Fourth, individuals are more likely to keep promises they make voluntarily and explicitly. The message for managers here is to get commitments in writing. Fifth, studies show that people really do defer to experts. So before they attempt to exert influence, executives should take pains to establish their own expertise and not assume that it's self-evident. Finally, people want more of a commodity when it's scarce; it follows, then, that exclusive information is more persuasive than widely available data.

By mastering these principles—and, the author stresses, using them judiciously and ethically—executives can learn the elusive art of capturing an audience, swaying the undecided, and converting the opposition.

A LUCKY FEW HAVE IT; most of us do not. A handful of gifted "naturals" simply know how to capture an audience, sway the undecided, and convert the opposition. Watching these masters of persuasion work their magic is at once impressive and frustrating. What's impressive is not just the easy way they use charisma and eloquence to convince others to do as they ask. It's also how eager those others are to do what's requested of them, as if the persuasion itself were a favor they couldn't wait to repay.

The frustrating part of the experience is that these born persuaders are often unable to account for their remarkable skill or pass it on to others. Their way with people is an art, and artists as a rule are far better at doing than at explaining. Most of them can't offer much help to those of us who possess no more than the ordinary quotient of charisma and eloquence but who still have to wrestle with leadership's fundamental challenge: getting things done through others. That challenge is painfully familiar to corporate executives, who every day have to figure out how to motivate and direct a highly individualistic work force. Playing the "Because I'm the boss" card is out. Even if it weren't demeaning and demoralizing for all concerned, it would be out of place in a world where cross-functional teams, joint ventures, and intercompany partnerships have blurred the lines of authority. In such an environment, persuasion skills exert far greater influence over others' behavior than formal power structures do.

Which brings us back to where we started. Persuasion skills may be more necessary than ever, but how can executives acquire them if the most talented practitioners can't pass them along? By looking to science. For the past five decades, behavioral scientists have conducted experiments that shed considerable light on the way certain interactions lead people to concede, comply, or change. This research shows that persuasion works by appealing to a limited set of deeply rooted human drives and needs, and it does so in predictable ways. Persuasion, in other words, is governed by basic principles that can be taught, learned, and applied. By mastering these principles, executives can bring scientific rigor to the business of securing consensus, cutting deals, and winning concessions. In the pages that follow, I describe six fundamental principles of persuasion and suggest a few ways that executives can apply them in their own organizations.

The Principle of Liking: People Like Those Who Like Them

The Application: Uncover Real Similarities and Offer Genuine Praise. The retailing phenomenon known as the Tupperware party is a vivid illustration of this principle in action. The demonstration party for Tupperware products is hosted by an individual, almost always a woman, who invites to her home an array of friends, neighbors, and relatives. The guests' affection for their hostess predisposes them to buy from her, a dynamic that was confirmed by a 1990 study of purchase decisions made at demonstration parties. The researchers, Jonathan Frenzen and Harry Davis, writing in the *Journal of Consumer Research,* found that the guests' fondness for their hostess weighed twice as heavily in their purchase decisions as their regard for the products they bought. So when guests at a Tupperware party buy something, they aren't just buying to please themselves. They're buying to please their hostess as well.

What's true at Tupperware parties is true for business in general: If you want to influence people, win friends. How? Controlled research has identified several factors that reliably increase liking, but two stand out as especially compelling—similarity and praise. Similarity literally draws people together. In one experiment, reported in a 1968 article in the *Journal of Personality,* participants stood physically closer to one another after learning that they shared political beliefs and social values. And in a 1963 article in *American Behavioral Scientists,* researcher F. B. Evans used demographic data from insurance company records to demonstrate that prospects were more willing to purchase a policy from a salesperson who was akin to them in age, religion, politics, or even cigarette-smoking habits.

Managers can use similarities to create bonds with a recent hire, the head of another department, or even a new boss. Informal conversations during the workday create an ideal opportunity to discover at least one common area of enjoyment, be it a hobby, a college basketball team, or reruns of *Seinfeld*. The important thing is to establish the bond early because it creates a presumption of goodwill and trustworthiness in every subsequent encounter. It's much easier to build support for a new project when the people you're trying to persuade are already inclined in your favor.

Praise, the other reliable generator of affection, both charms and disarms. Sometimes the praise doesn't even have to be merited. Researchers at the University of North Carolina writing in the *Journal of Experimental Social Psychology* found that men felt the greatest regard for an individual who flattered them unstintingly even if the comments were untrue. And in their book *Interpersonal Attraction* (Addison-Wesley, 1978), Ellen Berscheid and Elaine Hatfield Walster presented experimental data showing that positive remarks about another person's traits, attitude, or performance reliably generates liking in return, as well as willing compliance with the wishes of the person offering the praise.

Along with cultivating a fruitful relationship, adroit managers can also use praise to repair one that's damaged or unproductive. Imagine you're the manager of a good-sized unit within your organization. Your work frequently brings you into contact with another manager—call him Dan—whom you have come to dislike. No matter how much you do for him, it's not enough. Worse, he never seems to believe that you're doing the best you can for him. Resenting his attitude and his obvious lack of trust in your abilities and in your good faith, you don't spend as much time with him as you know you should; in consequence, the performance of both his unit and yours is deteriorating.

The research on praise points toward a strategy for fixing the relationship. It may be hard to find, but there has to be something about Dan you can sincerely admire, whether it's his concern for the people in his department, his devotion to his family, or simply his work ethic. In your next encounter with him, make an appreciative comment about that trait. Make it clear that in this case at least, you value what he values. I predict that Dan will relax his relentless negativity and give you an opening to convince him of your competence and good intentions.

The Principle of Reciprocity: People Repay in Kind

The Application: Give What You Want to Receive.
Praise is likely to have a warming and softening effect on Dan because, ornery as he is, he is still human and sub-ject to the universal human tendency to treat people the way they treat him. If you have ever caught yourself smiling at a coworker just because he or she smiled first, you know how this principle works.

Charities rely on reciprocity to help them raise funds. For years, for instance, the Disabled American Veterans organization, using only a well-crafted fund-raising let-ter, garnered a very respectable 18% rate of response to its appeals. But when the group started enclosing a small gift in the envelope, the response rate nearly doubled to 35%. The gift—personalized address labels—was extremely modest, but it wasn't what prospective donors received that made the difference. It was that they had gotten anything at all.

What works in that letter works at the office, too. It's more than an effusion of seasonal spirit, of course, that impels suppliers to shower gifts on purchasing departments at holiday time. In 1996, purchasing managers admitted to an interviewer from *Inc.* magazine that after having accepted a gift from a supplier, they were willing to purchase products and services they would have otherwise declined. Gifts also have a startling effect on retention. I have encouraged readers of my book to send me examples of the principles of influence at work in their own lives. One reader, an employee of the State of Oregon, sent a letter in which she offered these reasons for her commitment to her supervisor:

> *He gives me and my son gifts for Christmas and gives me presents on my birthday. There is no promotion for the type of job I have, and my only choice for one is to move to another department. But I find myself resisting trying to move. My boss is reaching retirement age, and I am thinking I will be able to move out after he retires. . . . [F]or now, I feel obligated to stay since he has been so nice to me.*

Ultimately, though, gift giving is one of the cruder applications of the rule of reciprocity. In its more sophisticated uses, it confers a genuine first-mover advantage on any manager who is trying to foster positive attitudes and productive personal relationships in the office: Managers can elicit the desired behavior from coworkers and employees by displaying it first. Whether it's a sense of trust, a spirit of cooperation, or a pleasant demeanor, leaders should model the behavior they want to see from others.

The same holds true for managers faced with issues of information delivery and resource allocation. If you lend a member of your staff to a colleague who is shorthanded and staring at a fast-approaching deadline, you will significantly increase your chances of getting help when you need it. Your odds will improve even more if you say, when your colleague thanks you for the assistance, something like, "Sure, glad to help. I know how important it is for me to count on your help when I need it."

The Principle of Social Proof: People Follow the Lead of Similar Others

The Application: Use Peer Power Whenever It's Available. Social creatures that they are, human beings rely heavily on the people around them for cues on how to think, feel, and act. We know this intuitively, but intuition has also been confirmed by experiments, such as the one first described in 1982 in the *Journal of Applied Psychology*. A group of researchers went door-to-door in Columbia, South Carolina, soliciting donations for a charity campaign and displaying a list of neighborhood residents who had already donated to the cause. The researchers found that the longer the donor list was, the more likely those solicited would be to donate as well.

To the people being solicited, the friends' and neighbors' names on the list were a form of social evidence about how they should respond. But the evidence would not have been nearly as compelling had the names been those of random strangers. In an experiment from the 1960s, first described in the *Journal of Personality and Social Psychology,* residents of New York City were asked to return a lost wallet to its owner. They were highly likely to attempt to return the wallet when they learned that another New Yorker had previously attempted to do so. But learning that someone from a foreign country had tried to return the wallet didn't sway their decision one way or the other.

The lesson for executives from these two experiments is that persuasion can be extremely effective when it comes from peers. The science supports what most sales professionals already know: Testimonials from satisfied customers work best when the satisfied customer and the prospective customer share similar circumstances. That lesson can help a manager faced with the task of selling a new corporate initiative. Imagine that you're trying to streamline your department's work processes. A group of veteran employees is resisting. Rather than try to convince the employees of the move's merits yourself, ask an old-timer who supports the initiative to speak up for it at a team meeting. The compatriot's testimony stands a much better chance of convincing the group than yet another speech from the boss. Stated simply, influence is often best exerted horizontally rather than vertically.

The Principle of Consistency: People Align with Their Clear Commitments

The Application: Make Their Commitments Active, Public, and Voluntary. Liking is a powerful force, but the work of persuasion involves more than simply making people feel warmly toward you, your idea, or your product. People need not only to like you but to feel committed to what you want them to do. Good turns are one reliable way to make people feel obligated to you. Another is to win a public commitment from them.

My own research has demonstrated that most people, once they take a stand or go on record in favor of a position, prefer to stick to it. Other studies reinforce that

finding and go on to show how even a small, seemingly
trivial commitment can have a powerful effect on future
actions. Israeli researchers writing in 1983 in the *Personality and Social Psychology Bulletin* recounted how they
asked half the residents of a large apartment complex to
sign a petition favoring the establishment of a recreation
center for the handicapped. The cause was good and the
request was small, so almost everyone who was asked
agreed to sign. Two weeks later, on National Collection
Day for the Handicapped, all residents of the complex
were approached at home and asked to give to the cause.
A little more than half of those who were not asked to
sign the petition made a contribution. But an astounding
92% of those who did sign donated money. The residents
of the apartment complex felt obligated to live up to
their commitments because those commitments were
active, public, and voluntary. These three features are
worth considering separately.

There's strong empirical evidence to show that a
choice made actively—one that's spoken out loud or
written down or otherwise made explicit—is considerably more likely to direct someone's future conduct than
the same choice left unspoken. Writing in 1996 in the
Personality and Social Psychology Bulletin, Delia Cioffi
and Randy Garner described an experiment in which college students in one group were asked to fill out a
printed form saying they wished to volunteer for an AIDS
education project in the public schools. Students in
another group volunteered for the same project by leaving blank a form stating that they didn't want to participate. A few days later, when the volunteers reported for
duty, 74% of those who showed up were students from
the group that signaled their commitment by filling out
the form.

The implications are clear for a manager who wants to persuade a subordinate to follow some particular course of action: Get it in writing. Let's suppose you want your employee to submit reports in a more timely fashion. Once you believe you've won agreement, ask him to summarize the decision in a memo and send it to you. By doing so, you'll have greatly increased the odds that he'll fulfill the commitment because, as a rule, people live up to what they have written down.

Research into the social dimensions of commitment suggests that written statements become even more powerful when they're made public. In a classic experiment, described in 1955 in the *Journal of Abnormal and Social Psychology,* college students were asked to estimate the length of lines projected on a screen. Some students were asked to write down their choices on a piece of paper, sign it, and hand the paper to the experimenter. Others wrote their choices on an erasable slate, then erased the slate immediately. Still others were instructed to keep their decisions to themselves.

The experimenters then presented all three groups with evidence that their initial choices may have been wrong. Those who had merely kept their decisions in their heads were the most likely to reconsider their original estimates. More loyal to their first guesses were the students in the group who had written them down and immediately erased them. But by a wide margin, the ones most reluctant to shift from their original choices were those who had signed and handed them to the researcher.

This experiment highlights how much most people wish to appear consistent to others. Consider again the matter of the employee who has been submitting late reports. Recognizing the power of this desire, you should, once you've successfully convinced him of the need to be more timely, reinforce the commitment by making sure it gets a public airing. One way to do that would be to send the employee an e-mail that reads, "I think your plan is just what we need. I showed it to Diane in manufacturing and Phil in shipping, and they thought it was right on target, too." Whatever way such commitments are formalized, they should never be like the New Year's resolutions people privately make and then abandon with no one the wiser. They should be publicly made and visibly posted.

More than 300 years ago, Samuel Butler wrote a couplet that explains succinctly why commitments must be voluntary to be lasting and effective: "He that complies against his will/Is of his own opinion still." If an undertaking is forced, coerced, or imposed from the outside, it's not a commitment; it's an unwelcome burden. Think how you would react if your boss pressured you to donate to the campaign of a political candidate. Would that make you more apt to opt for that candidate in the privacy of a voting booth? Not likely. In fact, in their 1981 book *Psychological Reactance* (Academic Press), Sharon S. Brehm and Jack W. Brehm present data that suggest you'd vote the opposite way just to express your resentment of the boss's coercion.

This kind of backlash can occur in the office, too. Let's return again to that tardy employee. If you want to produce an enduring change in his behavior, you should avoid using threats or pressure tactics to gain his compliance. He'd likely view any change in his behavior as the result of intimidation rather than a personal commitment to change. A better approach would be to identify something that the employee genuinely values in the work-place—high-quality workmanship, perhaps, or team spirit—and then describe how timely reports are consistent with those values. That gives the employee reasons for improvement that he can own. And because he owns them, they'll continue to guide his behavior even when you're not watching.

The Principle of Authority: People Defer to Experts

The Application: Expose Your Expertise; Don't Assume It's Self-Evident. Two thousand years ago, the Roman poet Virgil offered this simple counsel to those seeking to choose correctly: "Believe an expert." That may or may not be good advice, but as a description of what people actually do, it can't be beaten. For instance, when the news media present an acknowledged expert's views on a topic, the effect on public opinion is dramatic. A single expert-opinion news story in the *New York Times* is associated with a 2% shift in public opinion nationwide, according to a 1993 study described in the *Public Opinion Quarterly*. And researchers writing in the *American Political Science Review* in 1987 found that when the expert's view was aired on national television, public opinion shifted as much as 4%. A cynic might argue that these findings only illustrate the docile submissiveness of the public. But a fairer explanation is that, amid the teeming complexity of contemporary life, a well-selected expert offers a valuable and efficient shortcut to good decisions. Indeed, some questions, be they legal, financial, medical, or technological, require so much specialized knowledge to answer, we have no choice but to rely on experts.

Since there's good reason to defer to experts, executives should take pains to ensure that they establish their own expertise before they attempt to exert influence. Surprisingly often, people mistakenly assume that others recognize and appreciate their experience. That's what happened at a hospital where some colleagues and I were consulting. The physical therapy staffers were frustrated because so many of their stroke patients abandoned their exercise routines as soon as they left the hospital. No matter how often the staff emphasized the importance of regular home exercise—it is, in fact, crucial to the process of regaining independent function—the message just didn't sink in.

Interviews with some of the patients helped us pinpoint the problem. They were familiar with the background and training of their physicians, but the patients knew little about the credentials of the physical therapists who were urging them to exercise. It was a simple matter to remedy that lack of information: We merely asked the therapy director to display all the awards, diplomas, and certifications of her staff on the walls of the therapy rooms. The result was startling: Exercise compliance jumped 34% and has never dropped since.

What we found immensely gratifying was not just how much we increased compliance, but how. We didn't fool or browbeat any of the patients. We *informed* them into compliance. Nothing had to be invented; no time or resources had to be spent in the process. The staff's expertise was real—all we had to do was make it more visible.

The task for managers who want to establish their claims to expertise is somewhat more difficult. They can't simply nail their diplomas to the wall and wait for everyone to notice. A little subtlety is called for. Outside the United States, it is customary for people to spend time interacting socially before getting down to business for the first time. Frequently they gather for dinner the night before their meeting or negotiation. These get-togethers can make discussions easier and help blunt disagreements—remember the findings about liking and similarity—and they can also provide an opportunity to establish expertise. Perhaps it's a matter of telling an anecdote about successfully solving a problem similar to the one that's on the agenda at the next day's meeting. Or perhaps dinner is the time to describe years spent mastering a complex discipline—not in a boastful way but as part of the ordinary give-and-take of conversation.

Granted, there's not always time for lengthy introductory sessions. But even in the course of the preliminary conversation that precedes most meetings, there is almost always an opportunity to touch lightly on your relevant background and experience as a natural part of a sociable exchange. This initial disclosure of personal information gives you a chance to establish expertise early in the game, so that when the discussion turns to the business at hand, what you have to say will be accorded the respect it deserves.

The Principle of Scarcity: People Want More Of What They Can Have Less Of

The Application: Highlight Unique Benefits and Exclusive Information. Study after study shows that items and opportunities are seen to be more valuable as they become less available. That's a tremendously useful piece of information for managers. They can harness the scarcity principle with the organizational equivalents of limited-time, limited-supply, and one-of-a-kind offers. Honestly informing a coworker of a closing window of opportunity—the chance to get the boss's ear before she

leaves for an extended vacation, perhaps—can mobilize
action dramatically.

Managers can learn from retailers how to frame their
offers not in terms of what people stand to gain but in
terms of what they stand to lose if they don't act on the
information. The power of "loss language" was demonstrated in a 1988 study of California home owners written up in the *Journal of Applied Psychology*. Half were
told that if they fully insulated their homes, they would
save a certain amount of money each day. The other half
were told that if they failed to insulate, they would lose
that amount each day. Significantly more people insulated their homes when exposed to the loss language.
The same phenomenon occurs in business. According to
a 1994 study in the journal *Organizational Behavior and
Human Decision Processes,* potential losses figure far
more heavily in managers' decision making than potential gains.

In framing their offers, executives should also remember that exclusive information is more persuasive than
widely available data. A doctoral student of mine,
Amram Knishinsky, wrote his 1982 dissertation on the
purchase decisions of wholesale beef buyers. He observed
that they more than doubled their orders when they were
told that, because of certain weather conditions over-
seas, there was likely to be a scarcity of foreign beef in
the near future. But their orders increased 600% when
they were informed that no one else had that information yet.

The persuasive power of exclusivity can be harnessed
by any manager who comes into possession of information that's not broadly available and that supports an
idea or initiative he or she would like the organization to
adopt. The next time that kind of information crosses

your desk, round up your organization's key players. The information itself may seem dull, but exclusivity will give it a special sheen. Push it across your desk and say, "I just got this report today. It won't be distributed until next week, but I want to give you an early look at what it shows." Then watch your listeners lean forward.

Allow me to stress here a point that should be obvious. No offer of exclusive information, no exhortation to act now or miss this opportunity forever should be made unless it is genuine. Deceiving colleagues into compliance is not only ethically objectionable, it's foolhardy. If the deception is detected—and it certainly will be—it will snuff out any enthusiasm the offer originally kindled. It will also invite dishonesty toward the deceiver. Remember the rule of reciprocity.

Putting It All Together

There's nothing abstruse or obscure about these six principles of persuasion. Indeed, they neatly codify our intuitive understanding of the ways people evaluate information and form decisions. As a result, the principles are easy for most people to grasp, even those with no formal education in psychology. But in the seminars and workshops I conduct, I have learned that two points bear repeated emphasis.

First, although the six principles and their applications can be discussed separately for the sake of clarity, they should be applied in combination to compound their impact. For instance, in discussing the importance of expertise, I suggested that managers use informal, social conversations to establish their credentials. But that conversation affords an opportunity to gain information as well as convey it. While you're showing your dinner companion that you have the skills and experience your business problem demands, you can also learn about your companion's background, likes, and dislikes—information that will help you locate genuine similarities and give sincere compliments. By letting your expertise surface and also establishing rapport, you double your persuasive power. And if you succeed in bringing your dinner partner on board, you may encourage other people to sign on as well, thanks to the persuasive power of social evidence.

The other point I wish to emphasize is that the rules of ethics apply to the science of social influence just as they do to any other technology. Not only is it ethically wrong to trick or trap others into assent, it's ill-advised in practical terms. Dishonest or high-pressure tactics work only in the short run, if at all. Their long-term effects are malignant, especially within an organization, which can't function properly without a bedrock level of trust and cooperation.

That point is made vividly in the following account, which a department head for a large textile manufacturer related at a training workshop I conducted. She described a vice president in her company who wrung public commitments from department heads in a highly manipulative manner. Instead of giving his subordinates time to talk or think through his proposals carefully, he would approach them individually at the busiest moment of their workday and describe the benefits of his plan in exhaustive, patience-straining detail. Then he would move in for the kill. "It's very important for me to see you as being on my team on this," he would say. "Can I count on your support?" Intimidated, frazzled, eager to chase the man from their offices so they could get back to work, the department heads would invariably go along with his request. But because the commitments never felt voluntary, the department heads never followed through, and as a result the vice president's initiatives all blew up or petered out.

This story had a deep impact on the other participants in the workshop. Some gulped in shock as they recognized their own manipulative behavior. But what stopped everyone cold was the expression on the department head's face as she recounted the damaging collapse of her superior's proposals. She was smiling.

Nothing I could say would more effectively make the point that the deceptive or coercive use of the principles of social influence is ethically wrong and pragmatically wrongheaded. Yet the same principles, if applied appropriately, can steer decisions correctly. Legitimate expertise, genuine obligations, authentic similarities, real social proof, exclusive news, and freely made commitments can produce choices that are likely to benefit both parties. And any approach that works to everyone's mutual benefit is good business, don't you think? Of course, I don't want to press you into it, but, if you agree, I would love it if you could just jot me a memo to that effect.

Persuasion Experts, Safe at Last

THANKS TO SEVERAL DECADES of rigorous empirical research by behavioral scientists, our understanding of the how and why of persuasion has never been broader, deeper, or more detailed. But these scientists aren't the first students of the subject. The history of persuasion studies is an ancient and honorable one, and it has generated a long roster of heroes and martyrs.

A renowned student of social influence, William McGuire, contends in a chapter of the *Handbook of Social Psychology*, 3rd ed. (Oxford University Press, 1985) that scattered among the more than four millennia of recorded Western history are four centuries in which the study of persuasion flourished as a craft. The first was the Periclean Age of ancient Athens, the second occurred during the years of the Roman Republic, the next appeared in the time of the European Renaissance, and the last extended over the hundred years that have just ended, which witnessed the advent of large-scale advertising, information, and mass media campaigns. Each of the three previous centuries of systematic persuasion study was marked by a flowering of human achievement that was suddenly cut short when political authorities had the masters of persuasion killed. The philosopher Socrates is probably the best known of the persuasion experts to run afoul of the powers that be.

Information about the persuasion process is a threat because it creates a base of power entirely separate from the one controlled by political authorities. Faced with a rival source of influence, rulers in previous centuries had few qualms about eliminating those rare individuals who truly understood how to marshal forces that heads of state have never been able to monopolize, such as cleverly crafted language, strategically placed information, and, most important, psychological insight.

It would perhaps be expressing too much faith in human nature to claim that persuasion experts no longer face a threat from those who wield political power. But because the truth about persuasion is no longer the sole possession of a few brilliant, inspired individuals, experts in the field can presumably breathe a little easier.

Indeed, since most people in power are interested in remaining in power, they're likely to be more interested in acquiring persuasion skills than abolishing them.

Originally published in October 2001
Reprint R0109D

Moving Mountains

Executive Summary

WHAT COULD BE MORE FUNDAMENTAL to management, or more difficult, than motivating people? After all, a manager, by definition, is someone who gets work done through others. But how? A typical recipe for motivation calls for a mixture of persuasion, encouragement, and compulsion. Yet the best leaders, we suspect, need no recipe: They get people to produce great results by appealing to their deepest drives, needs, and desires. And so we discovered when we asked a dozen of the world's top leaders to describe how they each met a daunting challenge in motivating an individual, a team, or an organization.

Their answers are as varied as human nature. Some of the leaders appeal to people's need for the rational and the orderly: Mattel's Robert Eckert emphasizes the reassuring power of delivering a consistent message, and HP's Carly Fiorina focuses on facing hard truths and setting step-by-step goals. Some, like celebrated oceanographer Robert Ballard, Pfizer CEO Hank McKinnell, and BP America president Ross Pillari, see the powerful motivating effects of asking people to rise to difficult challenges. Others focus more on the human spirit, appealing to the desire to do something, as BMW's Chris Bangle puts it, "rare, marvelous, and lasting."

And quite a few inspire through example, as Dial chairman Herb Baum did when he donated $1,000 from his bonus to each of the company's 155 lowest-paid people. "If you draw the line on your own greed, and your employees see it," he says, "they will be incredibly loyal and perform much better for you." And he has the numbers to prove it. "Right now," he adds, "we're experiencing our lowest level of attrition in 11 years, and we're tracking toward another banner year because people are happy."

There's no trick to motivating others. It requires a clear, unbiased understanding of the situation at hand, deep insight into the vagaries of human nature at both the individual and the group levels, the establishment of appropriate and reasonable expectations and goals, and the construction of a balanced set of tangible and intangible incentives. It requires, in other words, hard thinking and hard work. And when an organization is under strain or is in crisis, the challenges—and the stakes—become that much higher.

The questions that managers have to grapple with as they try to inspire their people are many and complex: How do you deal with individuals or groups at different motivation levels that vary in different ways? How can you influence the behavior of a single individual, let alone an organization of hundreds or thousands? How can you help people feel enthusiastic and committed, especially in difficult times? To find out how such questions have been answered in practice, we asked nine business leaders—along with a high school teacher, an undersea explorer, and a champion sled dog racer—to describe how they met a daunting challenge in motivating an individual, a team, or an organization. Here's what they had to say.

Start with the Truth

Carly Fiorina is chairman and CEO of Hewlett-Packard in Palo Alto, California.

MY BIGGEST MOTIVATION CHALLENGE has been to reinvent HP in a way that celebrates its great history as a company while moving it forward. Doing that has required me to help people first to confront reality, then to set high aspirations, and finally to march pragmatically from reality to aspiration.

Honest confrontation is tough. I remember my first meeting with 700 of our senior leaders, when we underwent this very realistic self-appraisal about our customers, our competitive situation, and our performance. You can't do your own interpretation of what's wrong and beat people up; to motivate them to change, you have to show them a mirror. So on the white board, I wrote down comments these managers had themselves made two years earlier about the company, including the comment that HP was too slow and indecisive. I also wrote down things customers had said about us, both good and bad. When confronted with the inescapable facts of what they had said about themselves and what customers had told us, managers accepted the truth.

Once you have the truth, people need aspirational goals. To cross that uncomfortable gap between the truth and the goal, you must set very achievable, step-by-step measures. The process of doing begets progress; along the way, you must remind people of how far they've come already and how much closer they are to achieving the goal. That's when you see the light in their eyes. All these things—honest self-assessment, setting goals, and marching toward them—form a constant process, and they are also what make managing fun.

Appeal to Greatness

Christopher Bangle is global chief of design at BMW in Munich, Germany.

RECENTLY, MY DESIGN GROUP met a huge challenge—one that ended up inspiring the whole company. The new modern-art museum here in Munich—the *Pinakothek der Moderne,* which opened in September—invited BMW to put something on permanent display in time for the opening. Of course, doing any kind of installation demands a lot of time, and we didn't even hear about the offer until June. So I nixed the idea—we were too busy designing cars.

Our communications director begged me to reconsider, so I went to look at the museum space. Suddenly, I got excited by the idea of doing something truly grand. But to do it, I had to sell our board on the crazy idea of doing an enormously expensive, distracting design project that would bring in no revenue.

My argument went something like this: "Gentlemen, this is a once-in-a-lifetime cultural opportunity with the newest, largest design museum in Europe." Fortunately, art is a great motivator; the desire to contribute to something lasting is enormous. They approved, and we went to work. And work we did, with the kind of intensity and passion that comes with the knowledge that one is achieving something rare and marvelous.

Eighty days after first hearing of the project, 50 days after the board approved it, and 40 days after concept freeze, the museum opened with our gigantic installation, "The Art of Car Design." It's a lavishly shaped work occupying a 10×14 meter wall, consisting of 50 tons of milled Carrara marble, six screens displaying video loops, dynamic lighting, and more. On seeing it for the first time, one of the board members said to me, "Herr Bangle, you can be proud of this." And I replied, "No, you can be proud of this. You are a Medici."

Make Them Proud

2002 National Teacher of the Year, Chauncey Veatch works at Coachella Valley High School in Thermal, California.

M Y STUDENT "JOSÉ" SERVES AS a reminder of the power of motivation—which, for me, is about respecting my students and providing a way for them to contribute. Like so many of our students, José comes from a rural, migrant Hispanic family of modest means. He entered my American History class in the second semester of his

junior year as a special-education student. He had difficulty writing in English or Spanish and a history of frequent altercations at school. If he heard the word "fight,"
he deemed it an engraved invitation to participate, a
social event not to be missed.

The first step in motivating José was to celebrate the
gifts he brought to class. Though he had trouble writing,
he could speak cogently about concepts; our goal was to
help him get his thoughts on paper. He loved music, and
the poetry of rapper Tupac Shakur intrigued him, so we
tied his interest in rap music into our studies of the
American Civil Rights movement. At every mention of
the lyrics of contemporary music in the lesson, his ears
perked up.

José was given every opportunity to shine before his
peers. In an exam one day, I asked students to explain
one branch of government as laid out in the Constitu-
tion. He raised his hand and asked, "What's the name of
that French dude who wrote about the separation of
powers?" This was not a throwaway moment. So I asked
him to explain, and he responded, "You know, the idea
that the Congress, judges, and the president shouldn't be
more powerful than each other because if one branch
gets too strong it can become a dictator?" I stopped the
exam right there and said to the class, "José, the answer
to your question is Montesquieu—and you've just shown
you really understand a key point that I wish more
Americans understood." My entire class stood up and
applauded him. They knew what he had overcome.

Stick to Your Values

*L.M. Baker, Jr., is chairman of Wachovia in Charlotte,
North Carolina.*

MOST PEOPLE THINK motivating people is about
pushing others to do what you want them to do, but I've
found that the secret to motivating others has really
been to adhere to simple values, things like honesty, fairness, and generosity.

One of my biggest challenges was motivating myself
to go into business in the first place. I started out in life
thinking I was going to be a poet. I studied English in college but then found myself in Vietnam. By the time I got
out of the Marine Corps, the only things I knew how to
do were write poetry and conduct night combat patrols.
So I decided that to make a living I'd have to go to business school. At the time—this was 35 years ago—my wife
and I disapproved of what we saw as the power and
greed that often attend big business. When I took my
first job as a management trainee, we agreed that I could
give this business thing a try, but if either of us felt that
business was compromising our values, we'd leave it
behind. So I went to work in a commercial bank. All
these years later, I'm delighted to say I was never once
asked to compromise my own standards or values. That's
how I stay motivated, and that's how I strive to motivate
others.

Be a Broken Record

*Robert A. Eckert is chairman and CEO of Mattel in
El Segundo, California.*

PEOPLE CAN'T AND WON'T do much for you if no one
in the organization knows what's going on, what you
expect of them, and what the future holds. And talking

to them once a quarter isn't enough—you have to repeat messages of direction, inspiration, and comfort daily, in a variety of forms.

When I first got to Mattel, the company was in transition. In addition to spending major face time with all the senior managers, I spent hours and hours describing to all our employees and other stakeholders where we were going and how we were going to get there. I traveled and met with people, of course, but I also set up a program of regular e-mail updates, invited two-way communication, and responded personally to employee messages. Today, the company is back on track, but I'm still constantly communicating—in the elevator, in the cafeteria, on the street, on the phone, on planes, and through e-mails. And it's always the same basic message, which is our vision for the company.

I've found that this constant and consistent communication, while at times sounding like a broken record, is the single most reassuring thing I can do for all stakeholders: employees, investors, customers, media, and senior management. When employees hear what's going on from me first, they feel part of the team and most of all, respected, and that motivates them to come to work every day.

Build Trust

Susan Butcher is a four-time winner of the 1,150-mile Iditarod sled dog race.

WHEN I TALK ABOUT MOTIVATION, I'm not talking about people; I'm talking about motivating my sled dog team and each dog individually. Dogs are very intelligent, and you can't make them do anything they don't want to do. If they don't trust you, they won't go along with you.

My experience during the 1983 Iditarod is a good example. Back then, the trail was poorly marked, and I was a young musher. At one point, we got completely lost; I must have turned the team around 25 times over many hours looking for the trail. The dogs finally lost confidence in me. They'll forgive a few mistakes, but if you send them in the wrong direction too many times, they'll just stop. And that's what happened. With a lot of effort, I eventually convinced them to get moving. At times I had to walk in front of them for as much as 20 miles at a time. We finished in ninth place, after slipping below 20th. After we pulled into Nome, every single experienced musher told me that I'd never be able to use that team again, that the dogs would never recover their confidence. They thought the dogs had lost faith in themselves, but I knew they had lost faith in me.

So I set out to regain their trust. I taught them what "I'm sorry" means, so they'd know it was not their fault if I made mistakes. I simplified my commands so I could communicate with them even more clearly than I had before. And I put us into extremely challenging situations, so they learned that together we could always get out of trouble. At the same time, I let them know that I trusted them—that they could take the lead in the wilderness and challenge my commands if I put us in danger. For example, they're better than I am at spotting thin ice.

Over the course of the year, every dog regained full confidence in me and in the team. That same team took me to a very close second place the next year, and we went on to victory in 1986.

Encourage Risk

*Ross J. Pillari is the president of BP America in
Warrenville, Illinois, and is a group vice president
of London-based BP PLC.*

Helping people to try things that feel personally risky is the toughest motivational challenge. I experienced this firsthand when my own tolerance for risk was
tested in the early 1990s.

I was running BP's U.S. retail operation. At that time,
Lord Browne, BP's chief executive, asked me to be global
chief of staff for BP's research and engineering operation
and help it become more commercial. Browne thought I
was the right person to come in and help the group think
more like a business. I thought the new role was a terri-
ble idea.

I was a marketer, not a scientist; I couldn't speak the
language of science, and I certainly didn't have what I
thought was the skill set necessary to lead a group of
mathematicians and geologists. Why would I want to
risk my career by accepting a job where success seemed
so unlikely?

Browne didn't try to talk me into it. But he did get me
to talk openly about where I saw risks to myself and to
the organization. He also made it clear that I wasn't
assuming all the risk on my own. I accepted the job, and
we were successful in turning the R&D group into a
more commercially focused enterprise. Personally, it was
probably the most broadening assignment of my career.

What I learned from this experience and what guides
my thinking about motivation today is that you can't,
and you don't want to, eliminate all risks. But you can

help a person step into that slightly uncomfortable space where people and organizations achieve extraordinary results. The best way is through open and frank discussion about the likelihood of success, by making roles and accountabilities crystal clear, by spreading the risk across the team and the organization, and by providing visible and confident support regardless of the end result.

Care for the Little Guy

Herb Baum is chairman, president, and CEO of the Dial Corporation in Scottsdale, Arizona.

PEOPLE AT THE TOP of their organizations—the people who make the most money—often forget how hard it is for the people at the bottom. If the leader can make the people at the bottom feel like they're cared for, the entire organization will feel inspired and motivated.

My first CEO job was at Quaker State Corporation, which was headquartered in the little town of Oil City, Pennsylvania. The people who lived in this town and worked for the company lived modestly, and every dollar they earned mattered to them. I remember sitting with some of these folks and hearing how they went about buying even the most basic things, like shoes for their kids. After I heard that, I gave back the company car.

Today, the people at the bottom of my company are raising families on earnings of somewhere between $25,000 and $45,000 a year. Last year, they would have earned a bonus of about $500, while people at the top were making bonuses many times that size. So I went to the board and asked permission to give each of the 155 people who make the lowest salaries $1,000 from my own bonus. To me and most CEOs, $1,000 is a drop in the bucket. But for people trying to put a child through school or covering the health costs of a sick parent, it's a lot of money, and it helps.

If you draw the line on your own greed, and your employees see it, they will be incredibly loyal and perform much better for you. Right now, we're experiencing our lowest level of attrition in 11 years, and we're tracking toward another banner year because people are happy.

Ground Without Grinding

Mario Mazzola is the chief development officer at Cisco Systems in San Jose, California.

One of the hardest things about motivating others is creating a challenge that stimulates the energy and interest of bright people while keeping them anchored. If people are already reaching for the sky, you need to gently ground them without discouraging them.

On a personal level, I try to do this with my 13-year-old daughter. She has a penchant for mathematics and frequently will work ahead, something generally to be encouraged. But then she'll solve problems with more complex formulas than necessary. To encourage her to master the basics and learn the importance of simpler solutions, I will set her little problems that require her to include basic mathematical concepts, like derivatives. The idea is to give her a little challenge that also requires discipline, imagination, and self-confidence.

At work, I have another scenario. I manage a group of highly motivated, smart engineers who typically come up with the most efficient, innovative way to develop new technologies. The problem is that our customers work with existing technologies that require integration, which creates a much more complex problem. To keep the engineers from feeling frustrated at having to craft a more complex solution, I first genuinely acknowledge their ingenuity. Second, I have them meet with customers, so they can really understand and appreciate the customers' situations. That motivates them to drive through the homestretch and create technologies that are both innovative and meet current needs.

Leap First, Ask Later

Robert D. Ballard, whose team discovered the Titanic, the Bismarck, and PT-109, is the president of the Institute for Exploration in Mystic, Connecticut, and director of the University of Rhode Island's Institute for Underwater Archaeology at its Graduate School of Oceanography.

SOME PEOPLE THINK MOTIVATING people means coaxing, wheedling, and persuading them to adopt your point of view. But when the stakes are high or you're in an emergency, persuasion is out of the question. You just have to make the deal first, then figure out how to get there. When they realize there's no other way out, the team just gets the job done—and brilliantly.

We ran into a situation like this not long ago, when my team was preparing to film an underwater exploration at the Galápagos Islands for the Jason Project, which allows schoolchildren to view live dives from their classrooms. We had gathered $6 million in expensive telecommunication equipment, and the government of Ecuador offered to have its navy tow all of it to the islands for us. We accepted the offer, and then a week before we were to film, the barge sank 600 miles offshore.

A quarter-million schoolchildren had studied the Galápagos all year in preparation for this dive; to me, canceling the broadcast was totally out of the question. So we organized the biggest equipment scavenger hunt in existence. We divided 20 people into teams and got on the phones, gathering loans and donations from every possible source—universities, organizations, governments, individuals. I remember the CIA loaned us a plane. The team had all this stuff delivered to a warehouse in Miami, then flown to California and from there to Ecuador.

A week after the barge sank, we went live, on schedule, and all those school kids never knew the difference. As a result of this experience, the team knew it could do just about anything—and in very short order.

Set Different Incentive Levels

Liu Chuanzhi is chairman of Legend Group of Beijing.

OUR CHALLENGE HAS BEEN to motivate three distinctly different groups—executive team members, middle managers, and the rest of our line employees. We have different expectations for each group, and they each require different kinds of incentives.

Our executive team needs a sense of ownership in the company. Many state-owned enterprises in China face a special challenge: They cannot give their senior executives stock. But we took an untraditional approach; we reformed our ownership structure to make Legend a joint stock company, enabling us to give all our executive team members stock. In addition, senior executives need recognition, so we provide them with opportunities to speak to the media. To date, we've lost no senior executives to other companies.

Midlevel managers want to become senior managers, so they respond best to challenges—to opportunities to display and hone their talents. We set very high performance standards for our middle managers, and we let them participate in strategic processes, in designing their own work, and in making and executing their own decisions. If they get good results, they are handsomely rewarded.

Line employees need a sense of stability. If they take responsibility and are conscientious, they earn a predictable bonus. We also tie team performance to company or unit performance, and individual performance to team performance. For example, we might let the team decide how to allocate a percentage of their team bonus to individuals, with some general guidelines from the corporate level.

Work Quickly Through Pain

Hank McKinnell is the chairman and CEO of Pfizer in New York.

YOU MOTIVATE PEOPLE by moving quickly toward a goal, especially if getting to the goal involves pain. Knowing that the organization is committed to quick, decisive action frees people to think creatively and work in concert.

We saw this in the integration of Pfizer and Warner-Lambert in 2000. We won our bid for the company, but what we won was a firm thoroughly demoralized by a takeover battle. In my first meetings with the transition teams, I emphasized that we had to build a new company quickly, particularly before our largest competitor settled its own merger issues. The vision was ambitious—integrate Pfizer and Warner-Lambert, seek best practices where appropriate, and be ready to operate as a totally unified organization barely five months after the two companies agreed to the union.

Time was not our friend; our traditional approach of consensus building wasn't going to work. So we gave people permission to move fast and to make mistakes—as long as their actions were in keeping with our values of integrity, performance, and respect for people. The emphasis on speed tamped down resentment, turf issues, and "paralysis by analysis." In our U.S. sales force alone, for example, teams from both companies recommended more than 200 changes in operations and policies, and nearly all of them were accepted. Ultimately, hundreds of transition teams, composed of excellent people from both companies, knit together a nearly seamless new Pfizer that was totally operational just a few hours after signing the closing papers.

Originally published in January 2003
Reprint R0301B

Change the Way You Persuade

GARY A. WILLIAMS AND ROBERT B. MILLER

Executive Summary

YOU CALL A MEETING to try to convince your boss that your company needs to make an important move. Your argument is impassioned, your logic unassailable, your data bulletproof. Two weeks later, though, you learn that your brilliant proposal has been tabled. What went wrong?

It's likely the proposal wasn't appropriately geared toward your boss's decision-making style, say consultants Gary Williams and Robert Miller. Over the course of several years' research, the authors have found that executives have a default style of decision making developed early in their careers. That style is reinforced through repeated successes or changed after several failures.

Typically, the authors say, executives fall into one of five categories of decision-making styles: *Charismatics* are intrigued by new ideas, but experience has taught them to make decisions based on balanced information, not just on emotions. *Thinkers* are risk-averse and need as much data as possible before coming to decisions. *Skeptics* are suspicious of data that don't fit their worldview and thus make decisions based on their gut feelings. *Followers* make decisions based on how other trusted executives, or they themselves, have made similar decisions in the past. And *controllers* focus on the facts and analytics of decisions because of their own fears and uncertainties.

But most business presentations aren't designed to acknowledge these different styles—to their detriment. In this article, the authors describe the various subtleties of the five decision-making styles and how best to persuade executives from each group. Knowing executives' preferences for hearing or seeing certain types of information at specific stages in their decision-making processes can substantially improve your ability to tip the outcome in your favor, the authors conclude.

It's happened to you before. You call a meeting to try to convince your boss and peers that your company needs to make an important move—for instance, funding a risky but promising venture. Your argument is impassioned, your logic unassailable, your data bulletproof. Two weeks later, though, you learn that your brilliant proposal has been tabled. What went wrong?

All too often, people make the mistake of focusing too much on the content of their argument and not enough on how they deliver that message. Indeed, far too many decisions go the wrong way because information is presented ineffectively. In our experience, people can vastly improve their chances of having their proposals succeed by determining who the chief decision maker is among the executives they are trying to persuade and then tailoring their arguments to that business leader's decision-making style.

Specifically, we have found that executives typically fall into one of five decision-making categories: *Charismatics* can be initially exuberant about a new idea or proposal but will yield a final decision based on a balanced set of information. *Thinkers* can exhibit contradictory points of view within a single meeting and need to cautiously work through all the options before coming to a decision. *Skeptics* remain highly suspicious of data that don't fit with their worldview and make decisions based on their gut feelings. *Followers* make decisions based on how other trusted executives, or they themselves, have made similar decisions in the past. And *controllers* focus on the pure facts and analytics of a decision because of their own fears and uncertainties.

The five styles span a wide range of behaviors and characteristics. Controllers, for instance, have a strong aversion to risk; charismatics tend to seek it out. Despite such differences, people frequently use a one-size-fits-all approach when trying to convince their bosses, peers, and staff. They argue their case to a thinker the same way they would to a skeptic. Instead, managers should tailor their presentations to the executives they are trying to persuade, using the right buzzwords to deliver the appropriate information in the most effective sequence and format. After all, Bill Gates does not make decisions in the same way that Larry Ellison does. And knowing that can make a huge difference.

Five Approaches

Executives make it to the senior level largely because
they are effective decision makers. Learning mostly from
experience, they build a set of criteria that guides them.
Each decision is influenced by both reason and emotion,
but the weight given to each of these elements during the
decision-making process can vary widely depending on
the person.

In a two-year project, we studied the decision-making
styles of more than 1,600 executives across a wide range
of industries. Our work focused on how those people
made purchasing decisions, but we contend that the
results have broader applicability to decision making in
general. We interviewed participants about various
facets of their decision-making processes. For instance,
how strong was their desire to have others educate them
about the issues involved in a particular decision? How
willing were they to move beyond the status quo? How
much risk were they comfortable with in making the
decision? These characteristics and preferences are often
set early in a businessperson's career and evolve based
on experience. In other words, people have a natural tendency toward a certain style of decision making that gets
reinforced through successes—or that changes after
repeated failures.

Our research should not be confused with standard
personality tests and indicators like Myers-Briggs. Our
framework is simply a categorization of how people tend
to make decisions. Of course, people do not always make
decisions in the same way; much depends on the situation they're in. But our research has shown that when it
comes to making tough, high-stakes choices that involve
many complex considerations and serious consequences,

people tend to resort to a single, dominant style. Call it a default mode of decision making.

In this article, we describe each of the five decision-making styles in detail. This information is intended to be neither exhaustive nor definitive, and most executives will exhibit only some of the traits we list. Nevertheless, knowing the general characteristics of the different styles can help you better tailor your presentations and arguments to your audience. Unfortunately, many people fail in this regard. In our experience, more than half of all sales presentations are mismatched to the decision maker's style. Specifically, close to 80% of all sales presentations focus on skeptics and controllers, but those two groups accounted for just 28% of the executives we surveyed.

To investigate the various subtleties of the five decision-making styles, we present the following hypothetical situation. In each of the subsequent sections devoted to explaining the categories, we will use this tale to demonstrate how our fictional protagonist should best argue her case to her CEO.

MaxPro is a leading manufacturer of office equipment, including printers, photocopiers, and fax machines. The company has a centralized structure, with the bulk of its marketing and sales operations located at corporate headquarters. Mary Flood, the executive vice president of sales and marketing, knows she must restructure her operations to become more customer focused. Specifically, she needs to form major-account teams at the regional level instead of at the corporate level. All national accounts and targeted marketing would be based in one of five regions (Northeast, Southeast,

Five Styles of Decision Making—and the Ways to Influence Each

In our research, we found that executives typically have a default style of decision making that lands them in one of five distinct categories: charismatics, thinkers, skeptics, followers, and controllers.

From January 1999 to June 2001, we and our colleagues at Miller-Williams surveyed 1,684 executives to study their decision-making processes. The participants were from a range of industries (including automotive, retail, and high tech) and were interviewed by e-mail, in person, or over the telephone. The participants described their decision-making tendencies for our researchers—for instance, how long it took

	Charismatics	Thinkers
Description	Charismatics account for 25% of all the executives we polled. They are easily intrigued and enthralled by new ideas, but experience has taught them to make final decisions based on balanced information, not just emotions.	Thinkers account for 11% of the executives we surveyed and can be the toughest executives to persuade. They are impressed with arguments that are supported by data. They tend to have a strong aversion to risk and can be slow to make a decision.
Typical characteristics	enthusiastic, captivating, talkative, dominant	cerebral, intelligent, logical, academic
Prominent examples	Richard Branson, Lee Iacocca, Herb Kelleher	Michael Dell, Bill Gates, Katharine Graham
Buzzwords to use	results, proven, actions, show, watch, easy, clear, focus	quality, academic, think, numbers, intelligent, plan, expert, proof
Bottom line	When trying to persuade a charismatic, fight the urge to join in his excitement. Focus the discussion on results. Make simple and straightforward arguments, and use visual aids to stress the features and benefits of your proposal.	Have lots of data ready. Thinkers need as much information as possible, including all pertinent market research, customer surveys, case studies, cost-benefit analyses, and so on. They want to understand all perspectives of a given situation.

them to make a decision; their willingness to make a choice that might have negative consequences; their desire for others to educate them about the issues involved; and so on.

We performed a cluster analysis of these data and found that the executives' behaviors fell into the five groupings described on these two pages. The accuracy of the survey results reported in this article—for example, that 25% of the executives we interviewed were charismatics— is plus or minus 2.9%. For many of the prominent CEO examples cited, the categorizations are based on our firsthand observations and experiences with those executives; other categorizations are based on secondary sources, including media accounts.

Skeptics	Followers	Controllers
Skeptics account for 19% of the executives we polled. They tend to be highly suspicious of every data point presented, especially any information that challenges their worldview. They often have an aggressive, almost combative style and are usually described as take-charge people.	Followers account for 36% of all the executives we surveyed. They make decisions based on how they've made similar choices in the past or on how other trusted executives have made them. They tend to be risk-averse.	Controllers account for 9% of the executives we interviewed. They abhor uncertainty and ambiguity, and they will focus on the pure facts and analytics of an argument.
demanding, disruptive, disagreeable, rebellious	responsible, cautious, brand-driven, bargain-conscious	logical, unemotional, sensible, detail-oriented, accurate, analytical
Steve Case, Larry Ellison, Tom Siebel	Peter Coors, Douglas Daft, Carly Fiorina	Jacques Nasser, Ross Perot, Martha Stewart
feel, grasp, power, action, suspect, trust, demand, disrupt	innovate, expedite, expertise, similar to, previous	details, facts, reason, logic, power, handle, physical, grab, just do it
You need as much credibility as you can garner. If you haven't established enough clout with a skeptic, you need to find a way to have it transferred to you prior to or during the meeting—for example, by gaining an endorsement from someone the skeptic trusts.	Followers tend to focus on proven methods; references and testimonials are big persuading factors. They need to feel certain that they are making the right decision—specifically, that others have succeeded in similar initiatives.	Your argument needs to be structured and credible. The controller wants details, but only if presented by an expert. Don't be too aggressive in pushing your proposal. Often, your best bet is to simply give him the information he needs and hope that he will convince himself.

Midwest, Southwest, and West), each run by a different vice president. In Flood's plan, account executives for MaxPro's major customers (clients with revenues over $50 million) would relocate near the headquarters of those companies and would report directly to their respective regional VP. Each region would have its own marketing team and distribution channels, leaving corporate marketing responsible just for brand development. Flood needs to persuade George Nolan, MaxPro's CEO, to approve these changes.

1. Charismatics

Charismatics (25% of all the executives we interviewed) are easily enthralled by new ideas. They can absorb large amounts of information rapidly, and they tend to process the world visually.

They want to move quickly from the big idea to the specifics—especially those details regarding implementation. Charismatics are often described as enthusiastic, captivating, talkative, dominant, and persistent. They are risk-seeking yet responsible individuals. They are impressed with intelligence and facts and not usually given to self-absorption and compulsiveness. Prominent examples of charismatics include Richard Branson, Lee Iacocca, Herb Kelleher, and Oprah Winfrey. (Note that many of the categorizations of the executives we cite in this article are based on our firsthand observations and experiences with them. Some are based on secondary sources, including media accounts.)

Although charismatics may show great exuberance for a new idea, getting a final commitment from them can be difficult. They've learned from experience—particularly from the bad decisions they've made—to temper their initial enthusiasm with a good dose of reality. They seek out facts to support their emotions, and if such data can't be found, they will quickly lose their enthusiasm for an idea. Furthermore, charismatics prefer arguments that are tied directly to bottom-line results and are particularly keen on proposals that will make their company more competitive. They are rarely convinced by one-sided arguments that lack a strong orientation toward results. At the end of the day, charismatics make their final decisions very methodically, and the decisions are based on balanced information.

When trying to persuade a charismatic, you need to fight the urge to join in his excitement. One approach is to slightly undersell the parts of your proposal that pique his interest. In other words, you should be prepared to merely acknowledge the items that he greets with enthusiasm and discuss the risks of each of those things. This will ground your proposal in reality and strengthen his confidence and trust in you. You also need to keep the discussion focused on results. Your arguments must be simple and straightforward, and you should use visual aids to stress the features and benefits of your proposal. If you don't provide this results-oriented information (even when it's not asked for), you risk that the charismatic will not have it later when he needs it. Furthermore, you should be very honest and up-front about the risks involved with accepting your proposal, while also delineating the measures that can help minimize those risks. If you try to conceal any potential downsides, you can be sure that the charismatic will discover them later—when you're not available to address any concerns he may have.

All executives are busy people, but the attention span of a charismatic can be particularly short. In a meeting, you need to start with the most critical information. Otherwise, you risk losing his attention if you take your time leading up to a crucial point. Even if you have a two-hour meeting scheduled, you might not get through your entire presentation. Charismatics disdain canned arguments and will often interrupt you to get to the bottom line. Indeed, charismatics prefer highly interactive meetings; at times, they will want to move around the room and take control of the discussion.

Although charismatics might appear to be independent thinkers, they often rely on other high-profile executives in the company when making major decisions. Addressing this tendency will help increase your chances of success. Also critical will be your quiet perseverance: Charismatics expect you to wait patiently for them to make a decision, which could take some time, even though their initial enthusiasm may have led you to believe otherwise. Buzzwords that can help hold a charismatic's interest include: results, proven, actions, show, watch, look, bright, easy, clear, and focus.

PERSUASION IN PRACTICE:
NOLAN THE CHARISMATIC

Flood has scheduled an hour-long meeting with Nolan and the other members of the senior executive committee to discuss her proposed reorganization. Before that day, she previews her recommendations with COO Jack Warniers, Nolan's most trusted lieutenant. Warniers has several concerns about the restructuring, which Flood addresses and resolves through follow-up memos and e-mails.

Flood has prepared a few charts for the meeting, but these are merely for her own reference. Because she wants Nolan to feel like he can steer the discussion any which way, she will modify the charts in her head as necessary and redraw the information on a white board. Flood also knows that Nolan will at some point need all the details of the implementation—most of this information won't be discussed in the meeting—so she prepares a full report that she will give him afterward.

Flood starts her presentation by drawing a diagram that shows the current organization and its problems. Then she immediately jumps into her recommendations with a chart that outlines the new structure and how it will solve those problems. She emphasizes how the reorganization will increase MaxPro's overall competitiveness. "The restructuring," she says, "will help us to better focus on our customers, and the result will be fewer defections, particularly among our important accounts." She delineates how the reorganization will help propel MaxPro ahead of the competition.

Flood's ideas initially appeal to Nolan, who likes bold, out-of-the-box solutions, and he starts talking about the new restructuring as if it's already been accomplished. To keep him grounded, Flood outlines the potential impact of the new structure. Specifically, she notes the cost of relocating staff and the strong possibility that the change will meet fierce resistance from several groups, including the IT division, which would be responsible for supporting a large number of employees in remote locations.

Next, Flood presents a detailed risk assessment of the implementation—what will happen if the reorganization fails and the steps the company can take to minimize those risks. This information is as much for Nolan as it is for the others in the company who will be charged with implementing the plan. She then talks about the risk of doing nothing by highlighting evidence that at least three of MaxPro's major customers are already considering switching to a competitor because they are dissatisfied with MaxPro's customer service.

Knowing that the charismatic Nolan will want to move forward quickly, Flood ends her presentation by asking what their next steps should be. Nolan requests a detailed schedule, with milestone dates, of how the reorganization might progress. "I thought you might be interested in that information," she says, "so I've included it in this report, along with supporting data from the research we've conducted so far, case studies of similar reorganizations at other companies, and other pertinent facts. In particular, you might want to look at the section on risk assessment." Flood also tells Nolan that there are two versions of the report: an executive summary and an in-depth analysis. That night, on a red-eye flight to the East Coast, Nolan starts thinking about Flood's proposal and begins wondering how the restructuring will affect MaxPro's biggest customers. He turns to her report and finds that information in the table "Impact on Our Ten Largest Customers."

2. Thinkers

Thinkers (11% of the executives we interviewed) are the most difficult decision makers to understand and consequently the toughest to persuade.

They are often described as cerebral, intelligent, logical, and academic. Typically, they are voracious readers and selective about the words they use. They are impressed with arguments that are quantitative and supported by data. Not usually known for their social skills, thinkers tend to guard their emotions. They have two strong visceral desires in business—to anticipate change and to win—and they often pride themselves on their ability to outthink and outmaneuver the competition. They are driven more by the need to retain control than by the need to innovate. Prominent examples include Michael Dell, Bill Gates, Katharine Graham, and Alan Greenspan.

Thinkers have a strong desire for comparative data, which can make it difficult to persuade them. To make a decision, they need as much information as possible, including all pertinent market research, customer surveys, case studies, cost-benefit analyses, and so on. Perhaps the single-most important piece of information thinkers need is the presenter's methodology for getting from point A to point B. They strive to understand all perspectives of a given situation. And, unlike charismatics, thinkers have a strong aversion to risk.

When trying to persuade thinkers, your best approach is to openly communicate your worries and concerns about your proposal, because thinkers work best when they know the risks up front. Often they will ask a battery of questions to explore and understand all the risks associated with an option. Thinkers can be swayed when the arguments and presentation appeal directly to their intelligence. Interestingly, their thought process is very selective but not always completely methodical. They will, for instance, sometimes circumvent their own decision-making processes if they feel a bargain—a relatively low-risk opportunity to save time or money—is in their best interest.

Thinkers will never forget a bad experience, so you need to make sure that your recommendations to them are truly the best options. (Of course, you should do this for any of the five types of decision makers, but particularly so with thinkers.) And anyway, thinkers will eventually figure out for themselves whether something was truly the best alternative, so you might be better off refraining from drawing conclusions for them. Otherwise you'll risk being seen as too helpful and potentially not credible. One effective strategy for persuading thinkers is to give them ample time and space to come to their own conclusions.

In a meeting, thinkers will often take contradictory points of view. This can be extremely confusing, but remember that thinkers do not like to show their cards up front, so expect that you may not be able to discern how they feel about any of the options you present. In fact, thinkers often do not reveal their intentions until they render their final decisions. Furthermore, they can be self-absorbed, so be prepared for silence as they digest the information you've given them. Buzzwords and phrases that will capture a thinker's attention include: quality, academic, think, numbers, makes sense, intelligent, plan, expert, competition, and proof.

PERSUASION IN PRACTICE:
NOLAN THE THINKER

To convince Nolan, Flood knows she must present as many data, facts, and figures as possible, so her strategy is to deliver that information in huge chunks over a long-enough period of time for him to absorb and make sense of everything. Consequently, she decides that her best approach is to present her argument over the course of two meetings.

In the first, she begins by making her best case for why MaxPro needs to restructure. She emphasizes that if things stay the same, MaxPro will likely lose customers to competitors. (Interestingly, this piece of information—the risk of doing nothing—would be one of the last things she would present to Nolan if he were a charismatic. In fact, the order of presentation to a thinker is almost exactly the reverse order of presentation to a charismatic.)

Flood then explains how she arrived at the three options she has proposed for the restructuring. She details the methodology she used to gather and assess the data, and Nolan is quick to point out where she may have missed certain steps or made incorrect assumptions. This will benefit Flood in the long run, because Nolan is now taking ownership of her methodology.

Next, Flood highlights the pros and cons of each option, and she presents case studies of similar restructurings, including those from other industries and from different time periods. The case studies represent roughly an equal number of successes and failures. Flood points out why each was successful or why each failed, and from that she begins to write on a white board a list of reorganizing dos and don'ts, to which Nolan is quick to add his input.

Throughout her presentation, Flood is undaunted by Nolan's barrage of questions. She knows it's not a personal attack; it's an attack on her process or data. Flood is very up-front about where her data might be inconclusive or conflicting, where she's made assumptions using just her intuition, and areas where her argument is weak. Together, she and Nolan pick through the presentation. For one risk assessment that Flood has weighted as 60-40, for example, Nolan says it should be 50-50.

At the end of the first meeting, Flood draws up a to-do list that indicates where she needs to plug in more data or fill in gaps in her argument before the next meeting; Nolan helps her prioritize the list. In several instances, however, he says, "Well, I don't think we can get good data here, so let's just go by gut feel."

During the second meeting, Flood briefly summarizes what they discussed previously—with all the corrections and adjustments that Nolan has requested. Knowing that he hates surprises, she clearly points out anything new and different from the first presentation—for example, revised data. Next, using the updated information, she explains how she arrived at the optimum restructuring that maximizes the probability of success while keeping risks to an acceptable level. In conclusion, she shows the projected financial costs and additional revenues that the change will likely generate. After the meeting, Flood is prepared to wait weeks, if not months, for Nolan's decision.

3. Skeptics

Skeptics (19% of the executives we polled) are highly suspicious of every single data point, especially any information that challenges their worldview.

Perhaps the most defining trait of skeptics is that they tend to have very strong personalities. They can be demanding, disruptive, disagreeable, rebellious, and even antisocial. They may have an aggressive, almost combative style and are usually described as take-charge people. They tend to be self-absorbed and act primarily on their feelings. Prominent examples include Steve Case, Larry Ellison, and Tom Siebel.

During your presentation, a skeptic may get up and leave temporarily, take a phone call, or even carry on a side conversation for an extended period of time. He will be demanding of both your time and energy, locking horns with you whenever the opportunity arises. The thinker launches a volley of questions, and it is not personal; with a skeptic, it is. Do not let it get to you; just go through your presentation coolly and logically. The good news is that you will know almost immediately where you stand with skeptics. You can almost always depend on them to tell you what they are thinking because of their strong personalities.

To persuade a skeptic, you need as much credibility as you can garner. Skeptics tend to trust people who are similar to them—for instance, people who went to the same college or worked for the same companies. If you haven't established credibility with a skeptic, you need to find a way to have it transferred to you prior to or during the meeting—for example, by gaining an endorsement from someone the skeptic trusts. Doing this will let the skeptic maintain his superior position while allowing you to openly discuss issues on his level. Credibility can be transferred (from a colleague, for instance), but ultimately it must be earned, and you may have to go through some very aggressive questioning to establish it.

Challenging a skeptic is risky and must be handled delicately. Sometimes, to make your case, you will need to correct bad information that the skeptic is relying on. If, for instance, the skeptic states incorrectly that your company's R&D costs have been spiraling out of control recently, you might reply, "Are you testing me? Because I remember you telling me a couple months ago that we need to spend more to regain our leadership in developing innovative products. But maybe that's changed?" In other words, when you need to correct a skeptic, give him room to save face. For him to trust you, he needs to maintain his reputation and ego. And remember that skeptics do not like being helped; they prefer having people think they know something already.

Although persuading a skeptic might sound daunting, the process is actually very straightforward. Skeptics want to move forward with groundbreaking ideas, but they first need to make sure that those ideas are from people they fully trust. Skeptics usually make decisions quickly—within days, if not right on the spot. Buzzwords to use with a skeptic include: feel, grasp, power, action, suspect, trust, agreeable, demand, and disrupt.

PERSUASION IN PRACTICE: NOLAN THE SKEPTIC

Flood knows that she lacks the necessary clout to make her pitch directly to Nolan. So she enlists the aid of COO Jack Warniers, whom Nolan trusts. After she obtains Warniers's buy-in, she asks him to copresent the idea with her, hoping that his credibility will add to hers. They agree beforehand that Warniers will deliver all key messages, including the proposed restructuring and any data that might be controversial.

At the meeting, Flood and Warniers make their arguments in roughly the same order they would if Nolan were a thinker instead of a skeptic, but they emphasize the credibility of all their information sources. Flood knows that Nolan needs to hear things from multiple reputable sources—the more the better. So when discussing a recent marketing survey, she says, "I took the liberty of arranging a call between you and several other local market-research experts to discuss these results in greater detail." Whenever Nolan challenges anything, Flood and Warniers work quickly to ease his discomfort. Knowing that Nolan respects Bill Gates, for example,

Flood softens one of Nolan's attacks by saying, "I see your point, but you probably remember that Microsoft made a similar move about two years ago."

At every turn, Flood and Warniers are careful to tread lightly around Nolan's ego. When discussing the case studies, for instance, they introduce each one by saying, "You've probably seen this before . . ." or "As you know, Hewlett-Packard failed in a similar restructuring because. . . ." For each example, Flood and Warniers are quick to point out whether the company's image and reputation were enhanced or degraded as a result of the restructuring.

Because Nolan is particularly skeptical of anything abstract, Flood and Warniers are careful to make their arguments as concrete as possible, usually by grounding them in the real world. When they talk about relocating 200 employees, for example, they try to include the specifics: "We would need to close our building here on Hunter Avenue and sublease the space, including the adjacent parking lot. Because the building has a modular, funky layout, we might consider turning it into a business incubator."

At the end of their presentation, Flood and Warniers appeal to Nolan's rebellious streak by stating how the proposed reorganization would buck the trend in their industry. They also are quick to credit Nolan for inspiring the idea. "At the last meeting of the senior executive committee," Warniers says, "you talked about how we needed to ensure that we didn't lose touch with our customers. Your comment started us thinking about this restructuring." Flood and Warniers end their presentation with their proposed action plan for the reorganization, complete with a schedule of milestones. At that point, Nolan takes charge of the discussion.

4. Followers

Followers (36% of the executives we interviewed) make decisions based on how they've made similar choices in the past or on how other trusted executives have made them.

Because they are afraid of making the wrong choice, followers will seldom be early adopters. Instead, they trust in known brands and in bargains, both of which represent less risk. They are also very good at seeing the world through other people's eyes. Interestingly, despite their cautiousness, followers can be spontaneous at times. Above all, though, they are responsible decision makers, which is why they are most often found in large corporations. In fact, followers account for more than a third of all the executives we surveyed, representing the largest group among the five types of decision makers. Prominent examples include Peter Coors, Douglas Daft, and Carly Fiorina.

Followers may engage you in long lists of issues and repeatedly challenge your position (similar to what a skeptic does), but don't be fooled. In the end, they will agree to something only if they've seen it done elsewhere. But followers won't admit this. In fact, they will seldom concede that they are followers; they would much rather have you believe that they are innovative and forward thinking. Frequently, followers are mistaken for skeptics. However, followers are not inherently suspicious; they prefer that you help them gain a better grasp of what they don't understand. And although followers may exhibit a take-charge approach, they will yield when challenged. (As a general rule, people who are difficult to classify into a decision-making style are usually followers, because people in the other four groups tend to show their characteristics more definitively.)

Although followers are often the most difficult to identify, they can be the easiest to persuade—if you know which buttons to push. To obtain buy-in from a follower, you need to make him feel confident about deciding to move in a certain direction by proving that others have succeeded on that path. Not surprisingly, followers tend to focus on proven methods, and references and testimonials are big persuading factors.

With a follower, don't try to sell yourself unless you have a strong track record of success. Instead, look for past decisions by the follower that support your views or find similar decisions by other executives the follower trusts. Ideally, followers want solutions that are innovative yet proven, new but trusted, leading-edge yet somewhat safe. At the end of the day, though, what followers need most is to know that they won't lose their jobs. This is why they rarely make out-of-the-box decisions. In fact, for some followers, the only way to persuade them to adopt a truly bold strategy is to get someone else to do it successfully first. Buzzwords and phrases to use with a follower include: innovate, expedite, swift, bright, just like before, expertise, similar to, previous, what works, and old way.

PERSUASION IN PRACTICE: NOLAN THE FOLLOWER

Flood knows that her mission is simple: She must make Nolan feel comfortable that the decision to restructure has minimal risk. And to seal the deal, she must somehow also make him feel that he is being innovative.

In the meeting, Flood presents her arguments in
roughly the same order that she would if Nolan were a
thinker or skeptic. But because Nolan is a follower, Flood
emphasizes the case studies—eight of them in all. This
discussion resonates with Nolan because, like all
followers, he is particularly adept at placing himself in
others' shoes. As part of her strategy, Flood has decided
to omit any examples of failed restructurings—but she
has that information on hand, just in case Nolan asks for
it. The eight case studies are from industries outside of
MaxPro's business so that Flood can appeal to Nolan's
desire to be innovative by saying, "We could be the first
in our industry to do this kind of restructuring."

Next, Flood presents three options for the proposed
restructuring, and she links each of her case studies to
one of those options. To steer Nolan toward option three,
which she prefers, she has linked four of the cases to that
option; by contrast, she has provided Nolan with only
two case study references for each of the other two
options. When Nolan notes that option one is the cheap-
est, Flood is ready to address that issue head-on because
she knows how bargain conscious he is: Her detailed
analysis shows that, on a risk-adjusted basis, option
three is actually the least expensive because it is more
proven.

Presenting three options to Nolan does more than
just give him the opportunity to make a choice; it also
affords him the chance to be creative. He begins to combine aspects of options one and three—something Flood
had anticipated he would do. In fact, she has even
encouraged him to do so by presenting certain minor
components of the different options individually. For
Nolan, the ability to mix and match different parts of
proven strategies is perfect: It makes him feel innovative
without having to incur any major risk.

At the conclusion of the meeting, Flood further plays on Nolan's desire for both innovation and security by saying, "Yes, other companies have done this type of restructuring, but we will have more expertise implementing it, so we will do it faster and more cheaply. And because we already know what works and what doesn't, we'll be able to take the appropriate steps to avoid potential problems."

Flood understands that followers will maintain the status quo unless they're presented with information they can't afford to ignore. Because Nolan seems genuinely engrossed in hearing how the other companies have successfully reorganized, Flood expects she will hear from him within days. (Followers tend to act quickly once they see big potential for success with minimal risk.)

5. Controllers

Controllers (9% of the executives we surveyed) abhor uncertainty and ambiguity, and they will focus on the pure facts and analytics of an argument. They are both constrained and driven by their own fears and insecurities.

They are usually described as logical, unemotional, sensible, detail oriented, accurate, analytical, and objective. Like skeptics, controllers often have strong personalities and can even be overbearing. In their minds, they are the best salespeople, the best marketing experts, the best strategists, and so on. Whereas followers are good at putting themselves in others' shoes, controllers see things only from their own perspectives and will frequently make snap judgments and remarks that alienate others. Controllers can be loners and are often self-absorbed, traits that lead them to make unilateral decisions. Indeed, although a controller may talk to others about a decision, he will seldom genuinely listen to them or consider their input. Prominent examples include Jacques Nasser, Ross Perot, and Martha Stewart.

When dealing with controllers, you need to overcome their internal fears, which they will pretend they don't have. In fact, they will cover them up by paying an inordinate amount of attention to the intricate details of processes and methods. Dealing with controllers can be like playing a game of cat and mouse—you will always be chasing down some information at their request.

In a meeting, remember that controllers can be self-absorbed, so be prepared for long silences during your interactions. It is also crucial to remember that when cornered, controllers rarely capitulate. Furthermore, even though controllers seek accuracy and facts, that does not necessarily mean they will make intelligent, rational decisions. Often, a controller will jump to illogical conclusions. And unlike charismatics, who are willing to take responsibility for their decisions, controllers try to avoid being held accountable. When something goes wrong, they assume others are at fault.

To persuade controllers, your argument needs to be structured, linear, and credible. They want details, but only if presented by an expert. In practice, the only way to sell an idea to controllers is *not* to sell it; instead, let them make the choice to buy. Your best bet is to simply supply them with the information they need and hope they will convince themselves.

Although controllers and skeptics share several characteristics, a key difference is that controllers need ample time to make decisions (they hate to be rushed). By contrast, skeptics are much quicker on the draw. One of the worst things you can do with a controller is to push your proposal too aggressively. When that happens, controllers are likely to see you as part of the problem and not the solution. Buzzwords and phrases to use with a controller include: details, facts, reason, logic, power, handle, physical, grab, keep them honest, make them pay, and just do it.

PERSUASION IN PRACTICE: NOLAN THE CONTROLLER

Nolan is notorious for implementing only his own ideas, so Flood knows she must somehow make him take ownership of her proposed restructuring plan. To do that, she gears herself up for the long journey ahead. Over the course of several months, she continually sends him information—customer reports, marketing studies, financial projections, and so on—through all types of media (including print, video, and the Web) and in person. She needs to gently wear down his defenses by steadily supplying him with so much information that he simply has to make a decision.

First, Flood focuses on data that highlight MaxPro's problems because she knows that case studies and other information won't be as important to him. Her memos often prompt Nolan to request other information, sometimes arcane and irrelevant data. She gets this for him, knowing full well that he may not even look at it.

After four months she is tempted to schedule a formal presentation, but she resists the urge. Nolan himself must request that meeting. Until that time, she will have to be content with sending him still more information. When she does, she always provides the information in a structured, linear format. In a typical memo, she begins by writing, "Attached, please find the results from a recent customer survey, and here's how they fit in with the other material we have." Flood is also quick to point out (but not resolve) apparent contradictions in the data, knowing that Nolan prides himself in uncovering those kinds of inconsistencies. In one memo, she writes, "Here's some new research from Walker Consulting. It seems to contradict the study we commissioned last year. I'm not sure which to trust."

Finally, an event—the defection of one of MaxPro's largest customers—triggers action. Thanks to Flood's patient but incessant prodding, Nolan is sensitized to this latest development. He calls a meeting of the senior staff to discuss what MaxPro should do. Included will be a discussion of a possible reorganization.

CRITICS MIGHT VIEW some of our categorizations as derogatory—after all, few executives would like being classified as followers or controllers. We do not intend to imply that any decision-making style is superior to another; our labels are merely brief descriptors of the primary behavior of each group. In fact, each style can be highly effective in certain environments. Followers, for instance, have a high sense of responsibility and can be excellent leaders at large, established corporations. And controllers can be extremely effective business leaders; Martha Stewart is a case in point.

Furthermore, we do not mean to oversimplify the complex and often mysterious ways in which people reach conclusions. To be sure, decision making is a complicated, multifaceted process that researchers may never fully unpick. That said, we strongly believe that executives tend to make important decisions in predictable ways. And knowing their preferences for hearing or seeing certain types of information at specific stages in their decision-making process can substantially improve your ability to tip the outcome your way.

Originally published in May 2002
Reprint R0205D

Radical Change, the Quiet Way

DEBRA E. MEYERSON

Executive Summary

AT SOME POINT, many managers yearn to confront assumptions, practices, or values in their organizations that they feel are counterproductive or even downright wrong. Yet they can face an uncomfortable dilemma: If they speak out too loudly, resentment may build toward them; if they remain silent, resentment will build inside them. Is there any way, then, to rock the boat without falling out of it?

In 15 years of research, professor Debra Meyerson has observed hundreds of professionals who have dealt with this problem by working behind the scenes, engaging in a subtle form of grassroots leadership. She calls them "tempered radicals" because they effect significant changes in moderate ways.

Meyerson has identified four incremental approaches that managers can quietly use to create lasting cultural

95

change. Most subtle is "disruptive self-expression" in dress, office decor, or behavior, which can slowly change an unproductive atmosphere as people increasingly notice and emulate it. By using "verbal jujitsu," an individual can redirect the force of an insensitive statement or action to improve the situation. "Variable-term opportunists" spot, create, and capitalize on short- and long-term chances for change. And through "strategic alliance building," an individual can join with others to promote change with more force. By adjusting these approaches to time and circumstance, tempered radicals work subtly but effectively to alter the status quo.

In so doing, they exercise a form of leadership that is more modest and less visible than traditional forms—yet no less significant. Top managers who want to create cultural or organizational change—perhaps they're moving tradition-bound businesses down new roads—should seek out these tempered radicals, for they are masters at transforming organizations from the grass roots.

AT ONE POINT OR ANOTHER, many managers experience a pang of conscience—a yearning to confront the basic or hidden assumptions, interests, practices, or values within an organization that they feel are stodgy, unfair, even downright wrong. A vice president wishes that more people of color would be promoted. A partner at a consulting firm thinks new MBAs are being so overworked that their families are hurting. A senior manager suspects his company, with some extra cost, could be kinder to the environment. Yet many people who want to drive changes like these face an uncomfortable dilemma. If they speak out too loudly, resentment builds toward them; if they play by the rules and remain silent, resentment builds inside them. Is there any way, then, to rock the boat without falling out of it?

Over the past 15 years, I have studied hundreds of professionals who spend the better part of their work lives trying to answer this question. Each one of the people I've studied differs from the organizational status quo in some way—in values, race, gender, or sexual preference, perhaps (see the insert "How the Research Was Done" at the end of this article). They all see things a bit differently from the "norm." But despite feeling at odds with aspects of the prevailing culture, they genuinely like their jobs and want to continue to succeed in them, to effectively use their differences as the impetus for con- structive change. They believe that direct, angry con- frontation will get them nowhere, but they don't sit by and allow frustration to fester. Rather, they work quietly to challenge prevailing wisdom and gently provoke their organizational cultures to adapt. I call such change agents *tempered radicals* because they work to effect sig- nificant changes in moderate ways.

In so doing, they exercise a form of leadership within organizations that is more localized, more diffuse, more modest, and less visible than traditional forms—yet no less significant. In fact, top executives seeking to insti- tute cultural or organizational change—who are, per- haps, moving tradition-bound organizations down new roads or who are concerned about reaping the full poten- tial of marginalized employees—might do well to seek out these tempered radicals, who may be hidden deep within their own organizations. Because such individuals are both dedicated to their companies and masters at changing organizations at the grassroots level, they can prove extremely valuable in helping top managers to identify fundamental causes of discord, recognize alternative perspectives, and adapt to changing needs and circumstances. In addition, tempered radicals, given support from above and a modicum of room to experiment, can prove to be excellent leaders. (For more on management's role in fostering tempered radicals, see the insert "Tempered Radicals as Everyday Leaders" at the end of this article.)

Since the actions of tempered radicals are not, by design, dramatic, their leadership may be difficult to recognize. How, then, do people who run organizations, who want to nurture this diffuse source of cultural adaptation, find and develop these latent leaders? One way is to appreciate the variety of modes in which tempered radicals operate, learn from them, and support their efforts.

To navigate between their personal beliefs and the surrounding cultures, tempered radicals draw principally on a spectrum of incremental approaches, including four I describe here. I call these *disruptive self-expression, verbal jujitsu, variable-term opportunism,* and *strategic alliance building.* Disruptive self-expression, in which an individual simply acts in a way that feels personally right but that others notice, is the most inconspicuous way to initiate change. Verbal jujitsu turns an insensitive statement, action, or behavior back on itself. Variable-term opportunists spot, create, and capitalize on short- and long-term opportunities for change. And with the help of strategic alliances, an individual can push through change with more force.

Each of these approaches can be used in many ways, with plenty of room for creativity and wit. Self-expression can be done with a whisper; an employee who seeks more racial diversity in the ranks might wear her dashiki to company parties. Or it can be done with a roar; that same employee might wear her dashiki to the office every day. Similarly, a person seeking stricter environmental policies might build an alliance by enlisting the help of one person, the more powerful the better. Or he might post his stance on the company intranet and actively seek a host of supporters. Taken together, the approaches form a continuum of choices from which tempered radicals draw at different times and in various circumstances.

But before looking at the approaches in detail, it's worth reconsidering, for a moment, the ways in which cultural change happens in the workplace.

A Spectrum of Tempered Change Strategies

The tempered radical's spectrum of strategies is anchored on the left by disruptive self-expression: subtle acts of private, individual style. A slightly more public form of expression, verbal jujitsu, turns the opposition's negative expression or behavior into opportunities for change. Further along the spectrum, the tempered radical uses variable-term opportunism to recognize and act on short- and long-term chances to motivate others. And through strategic alliance building, the individual works directly with others to bring about more extensive change. The more conversations an individual's action inspires and the more people it engages, the stronger the impetus toward change becomes.

In reality, people don't apply the strategies in the spectrum sequentially or even necessarily separately. Rather, these tools blur and overlap. Tempered radicals remain flexible in their approach, "heating up" or "cooling off" each as conditions warrant.

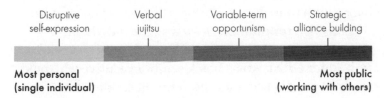

| Disruptive self-expression | Verbal jujitsu | Variable-term opportunism | Strategic alliance building |

Most personal (single individual)   Most public (working with others)

How Organizations Change

Research has shown that organizations change primar-ily in two ways: through drastic action and through evolutionary adaptation. In the former case, change is discontinuous and often forced on the organization or mandated by top management in the wake of major technological innovations, by a scarcity or abundance of critical resources, or by sudden changes in the regu-latory, legal, competitive, or political landscape. Under such circumstances, change may happen quickly and often involves significant pain. Evolutionary change, by contrast, is gentle, incremental, decentralized, and over time produces a broad and lasting shift with less upheaval.

The power of evolutionary approaches to promote cultural change is the subject of frequent discussion. For instance, in "We Don't Need Another Hero" (HBR September 2001), Joseph L. Badaracco, Jr., asserts that the most effective moral leaders often operate beneath the radar, achieving their reforms without widespread notice. Likewise, tempered radicals gently and continu-ally push against prevailing norms, making a difference in small but steady ways and setting examples from which others can learn. The changes they inspire are so incremental that they barely merit notice—which is exactly why they work so well. Like drops of water, these approaches are innocuous enough in themselves. But over time and in accumulation, they can erode granite.

Consider, for example, how a single individual slowly—but radically—altered the face of his organiza-tion. Peter Grant[1] was a black senior executive who held some 18 positions as he moved up the ladder at a large West Coast bank. When he first joined the company as a

manager, he was one of only a handful of people of color
on the professional staff. Peter had a private, long-term
goal: to bring more women and racial minorities into the
fold and help them succeed. Throughout his 30-year
career running the company's local banks, regional
offices, and corporate operations, one of his chief responsibilities was to hire new talent. Each time he had the
opportunity, Peter attempted to hire a highly qualified
member of a minority. But he did more than that—every
time he hired someone, he asked that person to do the
same. He explained to the new recruits the importance
of hiring women and people of color and why it was their
obligation to do likewise.

Whenever minority employees felt frustrated by bias,
Peter would act as a supportive mentor. If they threatened to quit, he would talk them out of it. "I know how
you feel, but think about the bigger picture here," he'd
say. "If you leave, nothing here will change." His example
inspired viral behavior in others. Many stayed and hired
other minorities; those who didn't carried a commitment
to hire minorities into their new companies. By the time
Peter retired, more than 3,500 talented minority and
female employees had joined the bank.

Peter was the most tempered, yet the most effective,
of radicals. For many years, he endured racial slurs and
demeaning remarks from colleagues. He waited longer
than his peers for promotions; each time he did move up
he was told the job was too big for him and he was lucky
to have gotten it. "I worked my rear end off to make
them comfortable with me," he said, late in his career. "It
wasn't *luck*." He was often angry, but lashing out would
have been the path of least emotional resistance. So
without attacking the system, advancing a bold vision,
or wielding great power, Peter chipped away at the

organization's demographic base using the full menu of change strategies described below.

Disruptive Self-Expression

At the most tempered end of the change continuum is the kind of self-expression that quietly disrupts others' expectations. Whether waged as a deliberate act of protest or merely as a personal demonstration of one's values, disruptive self-expression in language, dress, office decor, or behavior can slowly change the atmosphere at work. Once people take notice of the expression, they begin to talk about it. Eventually, they may feel brave enough to try the same thing themselves. The more people who talk about the transgressive act or repeat it, the greater the cultural impact.

Consider the case of John Ziwak, a manager in the business development group of a high-growth computer components company. As a hardworking business school graduate who'd landed a plum job, John had every intention of working 80-hour weeks on the fast track to the top. Within a few years, he married a woman who also held a demanding job; soon, he became the father of two. John found his life torn between the competing responsibilities of home and work. To balance the two, John shifted his work hours—coming into the office earlier in the morning so that he could leave by 6 PM. He rarely scheduled late-afternoon meetings and generally refused to take calls at home in the evening between 6:30 and 9. As a result, his family life improved, and he felt much less stress, which in turn improved his performance at work.

At first, John's schedule raised eyebrows; availability was, after all, an unspoken key indicator of commitment to the company. "If John is unwilling to stay past 6," his boss wondered, "is he really committed to his job? Why should I promote him when others are willing and able to work all the time?" But John always met his performance expectations, and his boss didn't want to lose him. Over time, John's colleagues adjusted to his schedule. No one set up conference calls or meetings involving him after 5. One by one, other employees began adopting John's "6 o'clock rule"; calls at home, particularly during dinner hour, took place only when absolutely necessary. Although the 6 o'clock rule was never formalized, it nonetheless became par for the course in John's department. Some of John's colleagues continued to work late, but they all appreciated these changes in work practice and easily accommodated them. Most people in the department felt more, not less, productive during the day as they adapted their work habits to get things done more efficiently—for example, running meetings on schedule and monitoring interruptions in their day. According to John's boss, the employees appreciated the newfound balance in their lives, and productivity in the department did not suffer in the least.

Tempered radicals know that even the smallest forms of disruptive self-expression can be exquisitely powerful. The story of Dr. Frances Conley offers a case in point. By 1987, Dr. Conley had already established herself as a leading researcher and neurosurgeon at Stanford Medical School and the Palo Alto Veteran's Administration hospital. But as one of very few women in the profession, she struggled daily to maintain her feminine identity in a macho profession and her integrity amid gender discrimination. She had to keep her cool when, for example, in the middle of directing a team of residents through complicated brain surgery, a male colleague would stride into the operating room to say, "Move over, honey." "Not only did that undermine my authority and expertise with the team," Dr. Conley recalled later, "but it was unwarranted—and even dangerous. That kind of thing would happen all the time."

Despite the frustration and anger she felt, Dr. Conley at that time had no intention of making a huge issue of her gender. She didn't want the fact that she was a woman to compromise her position, or vice versa. So she expressed herself in all sorts of subtle ways, including in what she wore. Along with her green surgical scrubs, she donned white lace ankle socks—an unequivocal expression of her femininity. In itself, wearing lace ankle socks could hardly be considered a Gandhian act of civil disobedience. The socks merely said, "I can be a neurosurgeon and be feminine." But they spoke loudly enough in the stolid masculinity of the surgical environment, and, along with other small actions on her part, they sparked conversation in the hospital. Nurses and female residents frequently commented on Dr. Conley's style. "She is as demanding as any man and is not afraid to take them on," they would say, in admiration. "But she is also a woman and not ashamed of it."

Ellen Thomas made a comparable statement with her hair. As a young African-American consultant in a technical services business, she navigated constantly between organizational pressures to fit in and her personal desire to challenge norms that made it difficult for her to be herself. So from the beginning of her employment, Ellen expressed herself by wearing her hair in neat cornrow braids. For Ellen, the way she wore her hair was not just about style; it was a symbol of her racial identity.

Once, before making an important client presentation, a senior colleague advised Ellen to unbraid her hair "to appear more professional." Ellen was miffed, but she didn't respond. Instead, she simply did not comply. Once the presentation was over and the client had been signed, she pulled her colleague aside. "I want you to know why I wear my hair this way," she said calmly. "I'm a black woman, and I happen to like the style. And as you just saw," she smiled, "my hairstyle has nothing to do with my ability to do my job."

Does leaving work at 6 PM or wearing lacy socks or cornrows force immediate change in the culture? Of course not; such acts are too modest. But disruptive self-expression does do two important things. First, it reinforces the tempered radical's sense of the importance of his or her convictions. These acts are self-affirming. Second, it pushes the status quo door slightly ajar by introducing an alternative modus operandi. Whether they are subtle, unspoken, and recognizable by only a few or vocal, visible, and noteworthy to many, such acts, in aggregation, can provoke real reform.

Verbal Jujitsu

Like most martial arts, jujitsu involves taking a force coming at you and redirecting it to change the situation. Employees who practice verbal jujitsu react to undesirable, demeaning statements or actions by turning them into opportunities for change that others will notice.

One form of verbal jujitsu involves calling attention to the opposition's own rhetoric. I recall a story told by a man named Tom Novak, an openly gay executive who worked in the San Francisco offices of a large financial services institution. As Tom and his colleagues began seating themselves around a table for a meeting in a senior executive's large office, the conversation briefly turned to the topic of the upcoming Gay Freedom Day parade and to so-called gay lifestyles in general. Joe, a colleague, said loudly, "I can appreciate that some people choose a gay lifestyle. I just don't understand why they have to flaunt it in people's faces."

Stung, Tom was tempted to keep his mouth shut and absorb the injury, but that would have left him resentful and angry. He could have openly condemned Joe's bias, but that would have made him look defensive and self-righteous. Instead, he countered Joe with an altered version of Joe's own argument, saying calmly, "I know what you mean, Joe. I'm just wondering about that big picture of your wife on your desk. There's nothing wrong with being straight, but it seems that you are the one announcing your sexuality." Suddenly embarrassed, Joe responded with a simple, "Touché."

Managers can use verbal jujitsu to prevent talented employees, and their valuable contributions, from becoming inadvertently marginalized. That's what happened in the following story. Brad Williams was a sales manager at a high-technology company. During a meeting one day, Brad noticed that Sue, the new marketing director, had tried to interject a few comments, but everything she said was routinely ignored. Brad waited for the right moment to correct the situation. Later on in the meeting, Sue's colleague George raised similar concerns about distributing the new business's products outside the country. The intelligent remark stopped all conversation. During the pause, Brad jumped in: "That's an important idea," he said. "I'm glad George picked up on Sue's concerns. Sue, did George correctly capture what you were thinking?"

With this simple move, Brad accomplished a number of things. First, by indirectly showing how Sue had been silenced and her idea co-opted, he voiced an unspoken fact. Second, by raising Sue's visibility, he changed the power dynamic in the room. Third, his action taught his colleagues a lesson about the way they listened—and didn't. Sue said that after that incident she was no longer passed over in staff meetings.

In practicing verbal jujitsu, both Tom and Brad displayed considerable self-control and emotional intelligence. They listened to and studied the situation at hand, carefully calibrating their responses to disarm without harming. In addition, they identified the underlying issues (sexual bias, the silencing of newcomers) without sounding accusatory and relieved unconscious tensions by voicing them. In so doing, they initiated small but meaningful changes in their colleagues' assumptions and behavior.

Variable-Term Opportunism

Like jazz musicians, who build completely new musical experiences from old standards as they go along, tempered radicals must be creatively open to opportunity. In the short-term, that means being prepared to capitalize on serendipitous circumstances; in the long-term, it often means something more proactive. The first story that follows illustrates the former case; the second is an example of the latter.

Tempered radicals like Chris Morgan know that rich opportunities for reform can often appear suddenly, like a $20 bill found on a sidewalk. An investment manager in the audit department of a New York conglomerate, Chris made a habit of doing whatever he could to reduce waste. To save paper, for example, he would single-space his documents and put them in a smaller font before pressing the "Print" button, and he would use both sides of the paper. One day, Chris noticed that the company cafeteria packaged its sandwiches in Styrofoam boxes that people opened and immediately tossed. He pulled the cafeteria manager aside. "Mary," he said with a big smile, "those turkey-on-focaccia sandwiches look delicious today! I was wondering, though . . . would it be possible to wrap sandwiches only when people asked you to?" By making this very small change, Chris pointed out, the cafeteria would save substantially on packaging costs.

Chris gently rocked the boat by taking the following steps. First, he picked low-hanging fruit, focusing on something that could be done easily and without causing a lot of stir. Next, he attacked the problem not by criticizing Mary's judgment but by enrolling her in his agenda (praising her tempting sandwiches, then making a gentle suggestion). Third, he illuminated the advantages of the proposed change by pointing out the benefits to the cafeteria. And he started a conversation that, through Mary, spread to the rest of the cafeteria staff. Finally, he inspired others to action: Eventually, the cafeteria staff identified and eliminated 12 other wasteful practices.

Add up enough conversations and inspire enough people and, sooner or later, you get real change. A senior executive named Jane Adams offers a case in point. Jane was hired in 1995 to run a 100-person, mostly male software-development division in an extremely fast-growing, pre-IPO technology company. The CEO of the company was an autocrat who expected his employees to emulate his dog-eat-dog management style. Although Jane was new to the job and wanted very much to fit in and succeed, turf wars and command-and-control tactics were anathema to her. Her style was more collaborative; she believed in sharing power. Jane knew that she could not attack the company's culture by arguing with the CEO; rather, she took charge of her own division and ran it her own way. To that end, she took every opportunity to share power with subordinates. She instructed each of her direct reports to delegate responsibility as much as possible. Each time she heard about someone taking initiative in making a decision, she would praise that person openly before his or her manager. She encouraged people to take calculated risks and to challenge her.

When asked to give high-visibility presentations to the company's executive staff, she passed the opportunities to those who had worked directly on the project. At first, senior executives raised their eyebrows, but Jane assured them that the presenter would deliver. Thus, her subordinates gained experience and won credit that, had they worked for someone else, they would likely never have received.

Occasionally, people would tell Jane that they noticed a refreshing contrast between her approach and the company's prevailing one. "Thanks, I'm glad you noticed," she would say with a quiet smile. Within a year, she saw that several of her own direct reports began themselves to lead in a more collaborative manner. Soon, employees from other divisions, hearing that Jane's was one of the best to work for, began requesting transfers. More important, Jane's group became known as one of the best training grounds and Jane as one of the best teachers and mentors of new talent. Nowhere else did people get the experience, responsibility, and confidence that she cultivated in her employees.

For Chris Morgan, opportunity was short-term and serendipitous. For Jane Adams, opportunity was more long-term, something to be mined methodically. In both cases, though, remaining alert to such variable-term opportunities and being ready to capitalize on them were essential.

Strategic Alliance Building

So far, we have seen how tempered radicals, more or less working alone, can effect change. What happens when these individuals work with allies? Clearly, they gain a sense of legitimacy, access to resources and contacts, technical and task assistance, emotional support, and advice. But they gain much more—the power to move issues to the forefront more quickly and directly than they might by working alone.

When one enlists the help of like-minded, similarly tempered coworkers, the strategic alliance gains clout. That's what happened when a group of senior women at a large professional services firm worked with a group of men sympathetic to their cause. The firm's executive management asked the four-woman group to find out why it was so hard for the company to keep female consultants on staff. In the course of their investigation, the women discussed the demanding culture of the firm: a 70-hour work week was the norm, and most consultants spent most of their time on the road, visiting clients. The only people who escaped this demanding schedule were part-time consultants, nearly all of whom happened to be women with families. These part-timers were evaluated according to the same performance criteria—including the expectation of long hours—as full-time workers. Though many of the part-timers were talented contributors, they consistently failed to meet the time criterion and so left the company. To correct the problem, the senior women first gained the ear of several executive men who, they knew, regretted missing time with their own families. The men agreed that this was a problem and that the company could not continue to bleed valuable talent. They signed on to help address the issue and, in a matter of months, the evaluation system was adjusted to make success possible for all workers, regardless of their hours.

Tempered radicals don't allow preconceived notions about "the opposition" to get in their way. Indeed, they understand that those who represent the majority perspective are vitally important to gaining support for their cause. Paul Wielgus quietly started a revolution at his company by effectively persuading the opposition to join him. In 1991, Allied Domecq, the global spirits company whose brands include Courvoisier and Beefeater, hired Paul as a marketing director in its brewing and wholesaling division. Originally founded in 1961 as the result of a merger of three British brewing and pub-owning companies, the company had inherited a bureaucratic culture. Tony Hales, the CEO, recognized the need for dramatic change inside the organization and appreciated Paul's talent and fresh perspective. He therefore allowed Paul to quit his marketing job, report directly to the CEO, and found a nine-person learning and training department that ran programs to help participants shake off stodgy thinking and boost their creativity. Yet despite the department's blessing from on high and a two-year record of success, some managers thought of it as fluff. In fact, when David, a senior executive from the internal audit department, was asked to review cases of unnecessary expense, he called Paul on the carpet.

Paul's strategy was to treat David not as a threat but as an equal, even a friend. Instead of being defensive during the meeting, Paul used the opportunity to sell his program. He explained that the trainers worked first with individuals to help unearth their personal values, then worked with them in teams to develop new sets of group values that they all believed in. Next, the trainers aligned these personal and departmental values with those of the company as a whole. "You wouldn't believe the changes, David," he said, enthusiastically. "People come out of these workshops feeling so much more excited about their work. They find more meaning and purpose in it, and as a consequence are happier and much more productive. They call in sick less often, they come to work earlier in the morning, and the ideas they produce are much stronger." Once David understood the value of Paul's program, the two began to talk about holding the training program in the internal audit department itself.

Paul's refusal to be frightened by the system, his belief in the importance of his work, his search for creative and collaborative solutions, his lack of defensiveness with an adversary, and his ability to connect with the auditor paved the way for further change at Allied Domecq. Eventually, the working relationship the two men had formed allowed the internal audit department to transform its image as a policing unit into something more positive. The new Audit Services department came to be known as a partner, rather than an enforcer, in the organization as a whole. And as head of the newly renamed department, David became a strong supporter of Paul's work.

Tempered radicals understand that people who represent the majority perspective can be important allies in more subtle ways as well. In navigating the course between their desire to undo the status quo and the organizational requirements to uphold it, tempered radicals benefit from the advice of insiders who know just how hard to push. When a feminist who wants to change the way her company treats women befriends a conservative Republican man, she knows he can warn her of political minefields. When a Latino manager wants his company to put a Spanish-language version of a manual up on the company's intranet, he knows that the white, monolingual executive who runs operations may turn out to be an excellent advocate.

Of course, tempered radicals know that not everyone is an ally, but they also know it's pointless to see those who represent the status quo as enemies. The senior women found fault with an inequitable evaluation system, not with their male colleagues. Paul won David's help by giving him the benefit of the doubt from the very beginning of their relationship. Indeed, tempered radicals constantly consider all possible courses of action: "Under what conditions, for what issues, and in what circumstances does it make sense to join forces with others?"; "How can I best use this alliance to support my efforts?"

CLEARLY, THERE IS NO ONE RIGHT WAY to effect change. What works for one individual under one set of circumstances may not work for others under different conditions. The examples above illustrate how tempered radicals use a spectrum of quiet approaches to change their organizations. Some actions are small, private, and muted; some are larger and more public. Their influence spreads as they recruit others and spawn conversations. Top managers can learn a lot from these people about the mechanics of evolutionary change.

Tempered radicals bear no banners; they sound no trumpets. Their ends are sweeping, but their means are mundane. They are firm in their commitments, yet flexible in the ways they fulfill them. Their actions may be small but can spread like a virus. They yearn for rapid change but trust in patience. They often work individually yet pull people together. Instead of stridently pressing their agendas, they start conversations. Rather than battling powerful foes, they seek powerful friends. And in the face of setbacks, they keep going. To do all this, tempered radicals understand revolutionary change for what it is—a phenomenon that can occur suddenly but more often than not requires time, commitment, and the patience to endure.

How the Research Was Done

THIS ARTICLE IS BASED ON A multipart research effort that I began in 1986 with Maureen Scully, a professor of management at the Center for Gender in Organizations at Simmons Graduate School of Management in Boston. We had observed a number of people in our own occupation—academia—who, for various reasons, felt at odds with the prevailing culture of their institutions. Initially, we set out to understand how these individuals sustained their sense of self amid pressure to conform and how they managed to uphold their values without jeopardizing their careers. Eventually, this research broadened to include interviews with individuals in a variety of organizations and occupations: business people, doctors, nurses, lawyers, architects, administrators, and engineers at various levels of seniority in their organizations.

Since 1986, I have observed and interviewed dozens of tempered radicals in many occupations and conducted focused research with 236 men and women, ranging from mid-level professionals to CEOs. The sample was diverse, including people of different races, nationalities, ages, religions, and sexual orientations, and people who hold a wide range of values and change agendas. Most of these people worked in one of three publicly traded corporations—a financial services organization, a high-growth computer components corporation, and a company that makes and sells consumer products. In this portion of the research, I set out to learn more about the challenges tempered radicals face and discover their strategies for surviving, thriving, and fomenting change. The sum of this research resulted in the spectrum of strategies described in this article.

Tempered Radicals as Everyday Leaders

IN THE COURSE OF THEIR daily actions and interactions, tempered radicals teach important lessons and inspire change. In so doing, they exercise a form of leadership within organizations that is less visible than traditional forms—but just as important.

The trick for organizations is to locate and nurture this subtle form of leadership. Consider how Barry Coswell, a conservative, yet open-minded lawyer who headed up the securities division of a large, distinguished financial services firm, identified, protected, and promoted a tempered radical within his organization. Dana, a left-of-center, first-year attorney, came to his office on her first day of work after having been fingerprinted—a standard

practice in the securities industry. The procedure had
made Dana nervous: What would happen when her
new employer discovered that she had done jail time for
participating in a 1960s-era civil rights protest? Dana
quickly understood that her only hope of survival was to
be honest about her background and principles. Despite
the difference in their political proclivities, she decided to
give Barry the benefit of the doubt. She marched into his
office and confessed to having gone to jail for sitting in
front of a bus.

"I appreciate your honesty," Barry laughed, "but
unless you've broken a securities law, you're probably
okay." In return for her small confidence, Barry shared
stories of his own about growing up in a poor county
and about his life in the military. The story swapping
allowed them to put aside ideological disagreements
and to develop a deep respect for each other. Barry
sensed a budding leader in Dana. Here was a woman
who operated on the strength of her convictions and was
honest about it but was capable of discussing her beliefs
without self-righteousness. She didn't pound tables. She
was a good conversationalist. She listened attentively.
And she was able to elicit surprising confessions from
him.

Barry began to accord Dana a level of protection,
and he encouraged her to speak her mind, take risks,
and most important, challenge his assumptions. In one
instance, Dana spoke up to defend a female junior
lawyer who was being evaluated harshly and, Dana
believed, inequitably. Dana observed that different standards were being applied to male and female lawyers,
but her colleagues dismissed her "liberal" concerns.
Barry cast a glance at Dana, then said to the staff, "Let's
look at this and see if we are being too quick to judge."

After the meeting, Barry and Dana held a conversation about double standards and the pervasiveness of bias. In time, Barry initiated a policy to seek out minority legal counsel, both in-house and at outside legal firms. And Dana became a senior vice president.

In Barry's ability to recognize, mentor, and promote Dana there is a key lesson for executives who are anxious to foster leadership in their organizations. It suggests that leadership development may not rest with expensive external programs or even with the best intentions of the human resources department. Rather it may rest with the open-minded recognition that those who appear to rock the boat may turn out to be the most effective of captains.

Notes

1. With the exception of those in the VA hospital and Allied Domecq cases, all the names used throughout this article are fictitious.

Originally published in October 2001
Reprint R0109F

Why People Follow the Leader

The Power of Transference

MICHAEL MACCOBY

Executive Summary

WE ALL ADMIRE LEADERS. In trying to understand how leadership works, however, we often lose sight of the fact that followers are a crucial part of the equation. Regrettably, they get short shrift in the management literature, where they are described as merely responding to their leaders' charisma or caring attitudes. What most analyses seem to ignore is that followers have their own motivations and are as powerfully driven to follow as leaders are to lead.

In this article, psychoanalyst, anthropologist, and management consultant Michael Maccoby delves into the unconscious recesses of followers' minds. He looks closely at the often irrational tendency to relate to a leader as some important person from the past—a parent, a sibling, a close friend, or even a nanny. Sigmund Freud discovered this dynamic when working with his patients and called it "transference." But as important as it is, the concept remains little understood outside the realm of clinical psychoanalysis. This is unfortunate, because a solid understanding of transference can yield great insight into organizational behavior and endow you with the wisdom and compassion to be a tremendous leader.

The author explains the most common types of transference—paternal, maternal, and sibling—and shows how they play out in the workplace. He notes that they have evolved as our family structures have changed. Whether followers perceive a leader as an all-knowing father figure, as an authoritative yet unconditionally loving mother figure, or as a brother or sister who isn't necessarily a model of good behavior, the leader can manage transferential ties by bringing unconscious projections to light. Then debilitating resentment and animosity can give way to mutual understanding and productivity—and a limping organization can start to thrive.

LEADERS, QUITE RIGHTLY, are the heroes of the corporate epic (a few leader-villains notwithstanding). They motivate us to go places that we would never otherwise go. They are needed both to change organizations and to produce results. In any business climate, good leadership is perhaps the most important competitive advantage a company can have. It's hardly surprising, therefore, that management scholars focus relentlessly on the attributes of successful leadership.

But in our understandable effort to grasp and master the skills of leadership, we tend to lose sight of the fact that there are two parts to the leadership equation. For leaders to lead, they need not only exceptional talent but also the ability to attract followers. Regrettably, however, it's becoming harder to get people to follow. The problem is that followers get short shrift in the management literature, where they are described largely in terms of their leaders' qualities. In other words, they're thought of as merely responding to a leader's charisma or caring attitude. What most analyses seem to ignore, though, is that followers have their own identity. Indeed, in 30 years of experience as a psychoanalyst, anthropologist, and management consultant, I have found that followers are as powerfully driven to follow as leaders are to lead.

Followers' motivations fall into two categories—rational and irrational. The rational ones are conscious and therefore well-known. They have to do with our hopes of gaining money, status, power, or entry into a meaningful enterprise by following a great leader—and our fears that we will miss out if we don't. More influential, much of the time, are the irrational motivations that lie outside the realm of our awareness and, therefore, beyond our ability to control them. For the most part, these motivations arise from the powerful images and emotions in our unconscious that we project onto our relationships with leaders.

Sigmund Freud, the founder of psychoanalysis, was the first person to provide some explanation of how a follower's unconscious motivations work. After practicing psychoanalysis for a number of years, Freud was puzzled to find that his patients—who were, in a sense, his followers—kept falling in love with him. Although most of his patients were women, the same thing happened with his male patients. It is a great tribute to Freud that he realized that his patients' idealization of him couldn't be traced to his own personal qualities. Instead, he concluded, people were relating to him as if he were some important person from their past—usually a parent. In undergoing therapy—or in falling in love, for that matter—people were transferring experiences and emotions from past relationships onto the present. Freud thought the phenomenon was universal. He wrote, "There is no love that does not reproduce infantile stereotypes," which, for him, explained why so many of us choose spouses like our parents.

Freud called the dynamic "transference," and it was one of his great discoveries. Indeed, for Freud, patients were ready to end therapy when they understood and mastered their transference. But even today, identifying and dissolving transferences are the principal goals of psychoanalysis.

But as important as it is, the concept remains little understood outside clinical psychoanalysis. This is unfortunate, because transference is not just the missing link in theories of leadership—it also explains a lot about the everyday behavior of organizations. A number of studies have shown, for example, that positive transferences are closely linked to productivity. Suppose an employee believes that her boss will care about her in a parental way. To ensure that this happens, she will make superhuman efforts to please her leader. As long as she perceives that these transferred expectations are being met, she will continue to work hard, to the obvious benefit of the organization as a whole.

The trouble is, not all transferences are positive. A worker might see his boss as someone he has to fight. And even if transference works well for a while, it can change quite suddenly if the employee's transferential expectations are not met. Consider Sylvia Hartman[1], a marketing manager in an East Coast market research and advertising company. Hartman was a creative but volatile employee who worked for Sam Phillips, a divisional vice president. Phillips took Hartman under his wing, and she soon came to value him as a mentor and friend. When a job that would have been a major promotion for Hartman opened up, she fully expected to get it. Instead, Phillips chose Harry Johnson, a move that devastated Hartman. She believed that she was vastly more intelligent than Johnson and had assumed that would be the primary basis for the promotion decision. However, Phillips said that he found Johnson to be more dependable and to have better people skills. When Hartman heard this explanation—and that Johnson would become her manager—she exploded in a destructive rage. She responded to her new boss by utterly ignoring his e-mails and phone calls, and she refused point blank to be supervised by him. Seeing the rift between his two players, Phillips thought about firing Hartman.

In doing psychoanalysis with Hartman, I found out that her rage was deeply rooted in her childhood. The eldest of five children, Hartman badly wanted to be her father's favorite. Hartman's father was a very successful executive, but he constantly disappointed her. Over and over again, he showed that he preferred one of her brothers to her, even though, in her view, the brother wasn't as smart as she was. Being passed over by Phillips evoked deep resentment in Hartman; it reopened a wound that had never healed. Hartman's transference of feelings from childhood to the workplace was unproductive. She could be a good "follower" to her boss only when she felt she was the favorite child. Unless she recognized her projections and worked them through, Hartman would be in danger of losing her job.

In consulting with companies as diverse as Volvo, AT&T, IBM, and ABB, I have seen countless cases like

Hartman's. But companies that might once have put up with this kind of leader-follower relationship cannot afford that luxury today. Transferences no longer necessarily work in leaders' favor, because to a large extent, the changing structures of families—more single-parent homes, dual working parents, and so on—have begun to create work environments where people value traditional leaders less. So it's time that leaders take the transference phenomenon seriously, learn how to mitigate its effects, and even manage it to the organization's advantage. In the following pages, I will explore the most common types of transference, showing how they can play out in the workplace and how they are evolving as the dynamics of family life change. Let's begin by examining the concept and dynamics of transference in more detail.

The Fantasy and the Facts

At its best, transference is the emotional glue that binds people to a leader. Employees in the grip of positive transference see their leader as better than she really is— smarter, nicer, more charismatic. They tend to give that person the benefit of the doubt and take on more risk at her request than they otherwise would. And as long as the leader's reality is not too far from the followers' idealization—and she doesn't start to believe in their idealized image of her—this works very well.

But without a strong grounding in reality, leaders can very easily come undone by their followers' positive transferential projections. At the extreme, such followers will create a myth that bears no relation to fact. A classic study of this dynamic is the movie *Being There*. In the film, Peter Sellers plays Chance the gardener, a simple man with little knowledge of the world beyond gardening. When his wealthy employer dies, Chance finds himself by happenstance socializing in the circles of the rich and famous. He behaves as he always has done, sharing his facile thoughts without considering their effect on those around him. But his new acquaintances start reading profound metaphors about politics and economics into his throwaway comments about gardening. By the end of the film, Chance is being touted as a U.S. presidential hopeful. Although few good leaders are so unaware of their impact that they will allow their relationship with followers to become this unrealistic, it's remarkable how often even reasonably self-aware leaders will become victims of illusion.

The transference dynamic is most likely to get out of control during periods of organizational stress. In such situations, followers tend to be more dominated by irrational feelings—in particular, the need for praise and protection from all-powerful parents. At the same time, the leader is preoccupied with handling the crisis at hand and, as a consequence, is probably less alert to the likelihood that his followers are just acting out childhood fears. This is what happened to a vice president of AT&T I was advising in the mid-1980s, during the breakup of the Bell System. While he was focusing on strategy, his followers felt frustrated that he was not dealing with their anxiety and reassuring them. Even though he was charting a promising new course for his division, employees complained that he wasn't leading them.

Another example of how transference is triggered by doubt and stress is the way people feel better just going to see a doctor, even before the doctor has done anything for them. In large measure, this phenomenon can be explained by patients' trust, which transfers the childhood experience of being cared for by parents when sick.

This type of transference makes it extremely hard for scientists to evaluate certain medications, such as mood-altering drugs. Clinical studies show, for example, that up to 30% of people respond as well to placebos—again, trust—as to antidepressants. People who volunteer for a study in hopes of finding a cure to their ailment may be especially receptive to placebos.

As well as being quite subtle in its workings, transference comes in many guises. It is blind to both age and gender, so stereotyping is very dangerous. A male leader, therefore, should never assume that he is a father figure or a brother figure—nor should a female leader assume she's a mother or a sister. Psychoanalysis has clearly shown that someone can have a paternal transference with a woman in authority and a maternal transference with a man.

What's more, the images we project from childhood are shaped by the family cultures we grew up with, a fact of particular importance today because more people now have family experiences that differ—sometimes quite radically—from what was long considered the norm. Indeed, I've noticed that for an increasing number of people, the significant person from the past is not a parent but a sibling, a close childhood friend, or even a nanny. Organizations are adjusting to the times, moving from hierarchies that worked well with parent-focused employees to more-horizontal setups that suit people who relate better to near equals. As we'll discuss later, the shift from parental to sibling transferences can fit organizations' needs for boundary-crossing project teams and networks. When managers at Boeing sought a leader for a software team that required a lot of interactivity among members, for instance, they joked about finding someone who was the fifth child in a family of ten siblings, someone who was used to mediating among brothers and sisters. In other words, the job called for a different kind of leadership than the traditional hierarchical boss would provide. Sibling leaders have to facilitate problem solving and build consensus.

Another complicating factor is that people can have multiple transferential relationships in an organization. It seems very likely to me that at General Electric over the past two decades, many employees not only had such relationships with their immediate bosses but also transferred childhood feelings onto Jack Welch, even though they had never met him. In cases of multiple transferences, both the immediate boss and the CEO might be seen as father figures. But when this happens, the employee usually experiences the transferences differently. Typically he will relate to his immediate boss from the perspective of a child who is four, five, or even older. But he will regard the CEO as a baby would see an earlier father figure, who is distant, protective, and all knowing.

Perhaps the biggest risk in transference comes from the fact that it is always a two-way street. Just as a follower projects his past experiences onto his leader, the leader responds by projecting her past experiences back onto the follower. Freud called this phenomenon countertransference and saw it as one of the most serious obstacles to resolving patients' psychological issues. The danger was that a psychoanalyst would respond to a patient's transferential protestations of love by accepting that love as real. As a result, the analyst might assume the role of a protective parent, furthering the patient's dependency. Or the analysis might end in a love affair rather than a cure. Countertransference is at least as big a problem for business leaders as for psychoanalysts. In his novel *Disclosure,* Michael Crichton describes how a

ruthless and dishonest woman is promoted above a
more-qualified man because she reminds the CEO of a
favorite daughter who was killed in an auto accident.
The CEO does not see her as she is but responds to her as
though she were his beloved daughter.

On the one hand, transference is a facilitator of fol-
lowership and therefore a source of strength for leaders;
on the other hand, it is a real threat to leaders because it
destroys objectivity. This is why, as we'll see, a good CEO
will try to understand transference and will work hard to
help his executive team members see one another as they
really are. The future of the company may depend upon
his ability to do so. It's worth taking time, therefore, to
examine the most common types of transference.

In the Name of the Father

The type of transference that Freud observed for the first
time was paternal transference, in which patients experienced unconditional love for the analyst as a wise, understanding, protective father. In such relationships with
Freud, patients slavishly gave up their own views and
embraced his as unquestionably correct. Paternal transference has been so prevalent in traditional corporations
that it has been considered normal behavior. In organizational surveys, people invariably describe their immediate
boss in positive terms, even when they express distrust in
top management. Indeed, the hierarchical structure of
traditional organizations has reinforced paternal transference. At every level in a hierarchy, individuals have a
boss who doles out assignments and rewards. This creates
in followers a willingness to obey orders—as well as an
overvaluation of the boss and a strengthening of infantile
wishes to be loved and protected.

My research shows that workers in paternalistically structured businesses typically see their boss from the perspective of a five-year-old boy who believes that "father knows best." Of course, even back in the 1970s, when I wrote a book on organizations called *The Gamesman,* different types of paternal transference could be found in business. Some people looked to their bosses as mentors, the kind of dads who introduced their sons to games and sports; others saw their bosses as demanding fathers whose approval was rarely (if ever) given. Perhaps the ideal paternal boss was the pipe-smoking, one-minute manager, the daddy figure who dispensed small doses of encouragement, approval, or constructive criticism, as needed. (See the insert "The Different Faces of Transference" at the end of this article.)

Whatever role followers project onto their leaders, most male CEOs in traditional organizations have consciously or unconsciously encouraged paternal transferences. They tend to show themselves in paternalistic settings—presiding over large meetings or smiling on videotapes—where the message is invariably reassuring, upbeat, hopeful. Even when times are bad, these leaders assure their followers that the downturn is temporary. The message is always the same: "Trust me to steer you through these troubled waters."

Some companies go a great distance to promote paternal transference. In the early 1970s, when I worked with managers at IBM, they told me that the company had a strict rule against teams and against shared decision making. The rule had come directly from the legendary CEO Tom Watson, Sr., and it had the effect of forging a direct link between employees and their bosses. Whether he was aware of it or not, Watson was sanctioning paternal transference at IBM. It was further reinforced by the company's paternalistic commitment to employees that good performance ensured lifetime employment.

I saw similar dynamics at work when I was a consultant to the executive team of AT&T Communications during the 1980s. Most of the vice presidents there were uncritically worshipful of their business unit presidents and the several CEOs who were making disastrous strategy moves—giving up cellular telephony, for instance, and losing billions in an effort to compete in computers. Instead of encouraging healthy debate about the future of the company, bosses expected—and rewarded—transferential veneration. I clearly remember one vice president who stuck out because he didn't comply with this company culture. Although his division produced the best results within the long-distance business unit, the executive team didn't appreciate him. This was not only because his realistic attitude toward his business unit's president was fraught with implicit criticism of other vice presidents' transferential over-valuation of the leader; it was also because he was an unconventional manager for AT&T at that time. Unlike the others, he delegated responsibility, didn't need to take credit for his division's successes, and initiated new businesses. Ultimately, he took early retirement, frustrated by his inability to push his ideas through the bureaucracy.

In this sort of environment, followers can find their trust in a benevolent leader to be sadly misplaced. Consider Eric Edwards, 27 years old and an executive assistant to the CEO of a prestigious international company. When he left this high-potential job, his colleagues and boss were extremely puzzled. He was taking a position at a lower salary with a much smaller company. And he didn't get stock options.

When asked why he was leaving, Edwards said he wanted to work with Ed Carey, a person he believed could teach him a great deal. He felt he shared a deep sense of mission with this older man, who had in the past gained considerable publicity for his innovations. At first, the work with Carey was productive and exciting, and Edwards basked in the credit Carey shared with him. But Carey had to be the innovator, the author of all the new ideas. He gave Edwards the role of implementer and invariably shot down or ignored Edwards's own ideas. It took five years of psychoanalysis before Edwards—who came from a traditional family—could realize that his attachment to Carey was transferential. As Edwards came to see, he initially had felt the same kind of support from Carey that he had once received from his father. Only when he saw that his boss did not treat him as a favored son but rather as a servant did Edwards seek to free himself. He told me that he'd learned a lot the first couple of years with Carey, but subsequent years on the job had been a waste of time.

For better or for worse, traditional paternal transference can create more loyal followers than any of the other forms of transference—in large part, because it tends to be a stable form of projection. Indeed, some of our best leaders are masters of manipulating the paternal transference of their followers. Movie director Francis Ford Coppola, for example, creates a family out of his cast members, who address him as "Papa" or "Godfather." Steven Spielberg's creative team calls him "Rabbi," which means "teacher." Both of these directors use the worshipful feelings of their casts and crews to pull out the dramatic performances that have resulted in some of the best films ever produced.

And of the Mother

Maternal transference differs from paternal transference in that it usually draws on an earlier childhood relationship. Unlike the father, who is often perceived as distant and detached, and whose approval is dependent on performance, the mother is often seen both as an authority figure and as a giver of unconditional love. She is the protective figure who gives us life and showers us with support, but she is also the first person who says no. It is the mother who weans us and, for the most part, who toilet trains us. Later it is she who separates herself from us to go back to work or to move on to other children. Not surprisingly, she is represented by both the fairy godmother and the evil stepmother in children's stories. She is both deity and witch, and this deep divide in our psyches can play itself out to dramatic effect in business situations. One only has to look at the public's extreme reactions of love and hate toward Martha Stewart to realize that women leaders stir up some of the most conflicted feelings we have in our unconscious.

Take, for instance, Jill Fisher and Allison Warren. Fisher, age 35, was vice president of the graphic design company founded by Warren, age 55. Both were creative and emotionally reactive. Warren was a mother figure whom Fisher counted on for unconditional love and support. When Warren felt that Fisher was sucking her dry, she withdrew emotionally, causing Fisher pain and confusion. Fisher felt like an adolescent who resents her mother because she still needs her. So any spark of disagreement could fire Fisher's anger, and the two would start screaming at each other. These confrontations caused Warren to take tranquilizers for anxiety attacks. Later, Fisher would abjectly apologize, and there would be mutual protestations of love. Of course, this was hard on Warren and upsetting to the other employees, who were sometimes brought into these transferential dramas.

Warren isn't the only strong woman to have a hard time of it in business. Think of Sherry Lansing, president of Paramount. Lansing is an ex-actress who, besides being beautiful, is brilliant and tall. She towers over the male subordinates she uses to convey bad news to movie hopefuls. In essence, she's taken on the role of Snow White to avoid being seen as the wicked witch. Even so, her underlings refer to her both as a goddess and as an ice queen. Tina Brown encountered similar ambivalence when she was the editor of the *New Yorker*. Followers often have a hard time dealing with strong women precisely because they stimulate in subordinates the feelings of awe and fear that the mother once did. Children depend on the help and support of the all-powerful mother. They also want her to be happy and proud of them, and they feel deep guilt if they cause her suffering—a fact that some mothers use to control their kids. Beneath the guilt is the unconscious fear that the mother will cut off her life-giving nurturance.

Maternal transferences generate greater expectations of empathy and tenderness from bosses than can realistically be met. Usually a boss's approval is more contingent, as it should be, on an employee's performance than on warm feelings. A colleague of mine saw this when he coached the 40-year-old vice president of a home-building company, who was told in no uncertain terms by the president that he had handed in a bad proposal.

The VP complained that the president should have shown more emotional intelligence in rejecting the proposal. When the president dismissed this complaint as "psychobabble," the VP grew irate. As my colleague immediately realized, the VP was projecting an inappropriate maternal transference. When the company's president didn't respond as the VP wanted, the VP reacted like a rejected child.

Positive maternal transferences can give people a powerful sense of support. Think of Ronald Reagan, whose wife, Nancy, was like a protective tigress during and after his presidency; he called her "Mommy." Although his father was a failed shoe salesman, Reagan's own strong mother was a major reason for his self-confidence and success. However, even positive maternal transferences can have bad effects. A close friend of mine taught for 18 years in a private school where most teachers had a maternal transference with the head-mistress, who created a family-like culture. The teachers loved their boss and felt cared for and protected by her, but the warm feelings they had were not a good measure of her ability to perform. As she neared retirement, the school was in the red, and it became clear that the head-mistress had done little either to evaluate and develop the teachers or to help them deal with discipline problems. While her successor was less comforting and more demanding, he succeeded in raising money from rich parents, improving teachers' salaries, and establishing rules that were followed.

Maternal transferences can sometimes be quite subversive of the formal organization even as they facilitate results. In one software company a colleague of mine consulted at, a number of male executives had a positive maternal transference with a woman coworker. She was the person they went to with their problems. These men were extremely competitive, but they were very comfortable communicating with one another through this woman. As one of the managers put it, "She doesn't have any hierarchical power, but she sure has network power." She was able to reassure the men that they could trust one another.

And Increasingly of the Brother

Sibling transference is as old as Cain and Abel, who competed for God's affection and attention, and Jacob and Esau, who competed for their father's. But over the past generation, sibling transferences have become less rivalrous and, at the same time, more influential. The rivalry has dissipated since children, increasingly raised in single-parent households or in families where both parents work, no longer care as much about being their parents' favorite. Instead, many of them develop close relationships at an early age with their siblings or with other kids in day care. As children cannot always rely on hardworking parents to be there when needed, they depend more on siblings and friends for emotional support. In fact, rather than trying to get what they want by pleasing their parents, kids learn at an early age to play on parental guilt and negotiate for privileges. Increasingly, these attitudes toward authority are being transferred to the workplace, making leadership even more difficult.

In the course of my research and consulting, I have consistently found that the employees who take most readily to horizontal organizations like cross-functional and project teams are those who were brought up in nontraditional families. Frontline employee Penny Nichols, for instance, a technician in her late twenties whom I met at an AT&T business service center, is comfortable interacting with her peer network. She's also developed independent relationships with customers—in one case, to the point where she personally controlled a multimillion-dollar account. This customer invites Nichols to conferences and refuses to deal with AT&T managers or account executives. I asked Nichols whether she felt comfortable handling this account by herself. She conceded that she did need assistance with some of the data, but her friend Annie Hellwarth from information services helped her out there. And what about her manager? What was his role? She said she needed his help only to get pricing information and to connect with other parts of AT&T when the company had new products she could offer the customer. But even though Nichols did a good job and was highly motivated, she was not fully qualified to develop the business relationship with the customer. Popular advice to management on empowering employees ignores this sort of problem. Employees like Nichols—who comes from a family where both parents worked and who not surprisingly has transferential ties to coworkers rather than to managers—function best as players in a game with clear roles, rules, rewards, and relations to authority. Otherwise, they tend to ignore authority, which can sometimes lead them to commit the company to bad deals.

Indeed, one consequence of the rise in sibling transference in leadership is that people are becoming increasingly critical of and ambivalent toward their bosses. At one company, I saw sibling transferences turn a group of employees into a band of brothers who were rebelling against an autocratic boss/father. People coming from nontraditional family cultures tend to evaluate bosses in terms of their value as leaders, which is very much the way children see team captains in the school yard. Thus, the newer generation of employees shows less interest both in being mentored and in mentoring, and more interest in developing reciprocal relations in their networks of peers.

Of course, these kinds of followers are hard to lead, for they often have an anarchic ideal of leadership. But their attitudes do fit the needs of the many companies that are moving away from product-based business models to total-solution strategies. To avoid narrowing profit margins, companies like GE Energy are wrapping products in services that require employees to work interdependently with customers. I consulted for ABB in Canada at a time when the company's electrical products were becoming commodities. To boost profits, we explored the potential of doing business with large customers like the zinc-mining and smelting company Cominco, which proposed partnering with ABB (rather than merely buying equipment) to increase energy efficiency and decrease environmental pollution. To pursue this opportunity, ABB had to pull people together from its different business units to work with engineers from Cominco.

Companies shifting from selling products to coproducing solutions recognize that they need to move away from traditional hierarchical models. Jay Galbraith, a professor at the University of Southern California, has written about this sort of shift at companies such as Nestlé, Nokia, and Citibank. He describes it in terms of forming cross-boundary networks that require leaders who can build trusting relationships to facilitate decision making and create consensus. IBM, once the poster child of hierarchy, is taking the lead in this change. The CEO, Sam Palmisano, is trying to move the company away from a pure hierarchy as he organizes to integrate technology with business processes. In IBM's latest annual report, Palmisano highlights promising opportunities in business transformation outsourcing, "which was not even part of the industry lexicon 18 months ago." Implementing IBM's new strategy will require teams of colleagues from different disciplines who are comfortable working together and willing to shift leadership roles according to who has the appropriate competence. There can be no clearer sign of the increased importance of sibling transferences.

Sibling transference has even made its debut in politics with the first baby boomer U.S. president, Bill Clinton. People didn't relate to Clinton as a father—the kind of transference you might have expected with the nation's commander in chief—but rather as an admired older brother or "buddy" (as Clinton named his dog). Although he had his critics, Clinton was never really expected to be a model of good behavior. Unlike Lyndon Johnson, for whom Americans' positive attitude flipped when their paternal-transferential expectations were shattered, Clinton was allowed to get away with his womanizing because he was perceived by much of the public as merely a naughty brother.

Making Transference Work for You

If all relationships are colored by transference, how can you ever know if your followers' relationships with you are real? The short answer is that you can't. Even the closest relationships combine objective reality with images and emotions carried over from the past, and there will never be any way around that. However, your followers' motivations for following don't have to be based in reality in order to work. What's more, there are ways of managing transferences that not only reduce the potential for negative transferences but actually increase the likelihood of positive ones.

A key way that managers can influence their followers' positive and negative transferences is to acknowledge their own transferences. The classic path to self-knowledge is introspection—the approach favored in psychology. The trouble with introspection, of course, is that it can paralyze a leader, especially one with a strong obsessive bent. Endless self-analysis will prevent her from making quick decisions. Consequently, many of the most effective leaders rely on an outsider to provide an incisive reality check. The "consultant" can be a member of the family—Bill Gates, for instance, routinely uses his wife as a sounding board. Other people turn to a longtime friend or associate, as British tycoon Lord James Hanson relied heavily on his U.S.-based business partner Sir Gordon White. Increasingly, leaders also work with executive coaches to get an outside view.

When leaders wish to manage followers' transferences, as well as their own, they can start by bringing the unconscious into awareness—which is what Freud is all about. This effort is especially important when staff members view a leader through different transferential lenses. In such a situation, a leader can deal with his followers' transferences by showing himself more as he actually is, thereby demystifying his professional relationships. But don't count on these steps to eliminate projections. So long as they are unconscious, transferences remain strong. What's worse, the positive transference of the follower is likely to become negative before it disappears, as we have seen in public attitudes toward U.S. presidents.

In consulting with CEOs, I've had them and their executive teams answer the personality questionnaire from my book *The Productive Narcissist* as a way to discuss how the personalities of the individuals influence their leadership style and how they relate to one another and their followers. This exercise has increased mutual understanding and objectivity, sometimes uncovering problematic transferences. In one case, it became clear that a chief financial officer was totally focused on pleasing the CEO, who was a father figure for her. She was resentful that the CEO didn't show her more attention; at the same time, however, she ignored several vice presidents who offered their help. The more people know one another and the rules of the game, the harder it is to project and the more obviously unreal the projections will be.

As the new CEO of DAI, an international development company struggling to manage its growth, Tony Barclay took precisely this approach in succeeding a father figure CEO. In order to prevent people from automatically relating to him as a patriarch or else resenting him as the brother who usurped the father, Barclay took a lot of time and trouble to make sure that all his employees knew him very well. He also went to great lengths to help them realize that their rewards and promotions depended on their own performance, not on their relationship with him. Barclay calls his style of leadership "management by consequence," and it essentially centers on building a mutual understanding between leader and follower.

Barclay's approach has not only mitigated negative transferences and childlike dependencies at DAI; it also has made Barclay into a role model for his managers and other employees. Becoming a role model strengthens a leader's authority and inspires teamwork and company spirit. We can see this dynamic at work in sports teams. Michael Jordan, especially when he was at his prime playing for the Chicago Bulls, was the unquestioned leader of a group of highly paid athletes who would not easily accept authority. Rather than expect Jordan to be a caring parent, teammates wanted to "be like Mike." The difficulty of the role-model approach is that you can't fake it. Employees have to see you as an authentic ideal, like Bill Gates or Steve Jobs. (Of course, you also need employees with enough talent and confidence to feel they can be like Bill or Steve.) Barclay says that sustaining this role takes a lot of work. "If you get lazy, you'll lose it."

The path to mutual understanding is often a long one, and organizations can implode before treatment strategies take effect. One way to speed things up a little is the time-honored tactic of creating an outside enemy. This provides a short-term boost to employees' positive transferences, allowing them to get over negative feelings about the leader, at least for a while. This approach strengthened the transferential following of George W. Bush after September 11, 2001, as he emphasized his leadership in protecting the United States from terrorist threats. (However, we have seen that this kind of transference can turn negative when leadership appears to fail.) Former CEO Goran Collert took the outside-enemy approach at Swedbank. He told employees that the bank faced threats not only from Swedish competitors but also from the Danes, the Dutch, and the Germans. The psychological impact of the threat—real or not—was to strengthen workers' positive transference with Collert as a leader. (See the insert "Managing Transference" at the end of this article.)

Effective as the outside-enemy tactic can be in buying a leader some time to understand and manage the transference problem, it does carry serious long-term dangers.

In time, insecurity and anxiety in the face of the outside threat can cause people to regress to a childlike state where they want their leader to protect them. They don't step up to responsibility, and their anxiety becomes corrosive to the organization. Additionally, when a leader starts acting like a general marshaling forces against the enemy, employees can become more afraid of the authoritative leader than of the external threat. Creating a common enemy, therefore, is a strategy that should always be used sparingly and never in isolation.

No LEADER WILL EVER BE ABLE to completely control his followers' unconscious motivations—transference is too deeply ingrained in human nature for that. Yet if the organization is to be protected from itself, followers' projections and motivations must be channeled and managed. The challenge is especially urgent for today's organizations, in which increasing diversity requires us all to move away from stereotyping and really understand differences in personality and ways of thinking and learning.

The Different Faces of Transference

WHEN I WAS A CONSULTANT TO ABB in the 1990s, I was asked to interview managers in Asia, Europe, and North America. My goal was to understand how local managers and expatriates viewed strategy, organization, and one another. I asked interviewees two questions: "What is your view of a good manager, and what is your view of a good father?" The answers were invariably related, but there was a sharp divide between the responses of Westerners and those of many Asians.

Westerners, particularly Americans and Scandinavians, viewed good fathers and good managers as people who were helpful when needed but who generally encouraged their followers to be independent. By contrast, the Asians—particularly the ethnic Chinese in Taiwan, Hong Kong, and Singapore—wanted a father-manager who protected them and taught them. In return, they were willing to give the leader complete loyalty and obedience. Not surprisingly, these Asians thought of Western leaders as bad parents who woefully neglected their children. However, young managers from Beijing, where the Cultural Revolution broke traditional family patterns, responded somewhat like the Westerners. They described the ideal leader as a good basketball coach who put people into the right roles, promoted teamwork, and knew how to adapt strategy to changing competition.

Differences between East and West are further amplified by the relative decline of parental authority in America. Managers from Asian and Eastern European companies still come from traditional families and thus tend to develop paternal transferences—so they often find it difficult to deal with American organizations, which are increasingly motivated by maternal and sibling transferences. And Westerners often fail to appreciate Asian and Eastern European organizations' need for leaders who reward loyalty with parental interest in their followers.

Managing Transference

IT IS IMPOSSIBLE TO MASTER your followers' transferences for them. Followers need to do that on their own—and in some cases, it can require years of therapy with a highly trained analyst. But you can safely guide them in the right direction by taking these three steps:

Know yourself.

Get constant reality checks from family, outsiders, and business associates. Build a team of close colleagues to help keep your perceptions grounded in reality.

Promote mutual understanding.

Make sure people know you. Share your foibles wisely. Don't pretend to be what you're not. Make sure everyone knows the rules that you play by and that you want them to play by.

Create a common enemy.

Buy time for self-knowledge and mutual understanding by rallying people against an outside threat. But make sure they don't feel too threatened and that you don't become too scary in the process.

Notes

1. I have changed the names and occupations in examples from my clinical work and that of my colleagues.

Originally published in September 2004
Reprint R0409E

What You Don't Know About Making Decisions

DAVID A. GARVIN AND
MICHAEL A. ROBERTO

Executive Summary

MOST EXECUTIVES THINK OF decision making as a
singular event that occurs at a particular point in time. In
reality, though, decision making is a process fraught with
power plays, politics, personal nuances, and institutional
history. Leaders who recognize this make far better
decisions than those who persevere in the fantasy that
decisions are events they alone control.

That said, some decision-making processes are far
more effective than others. Most often, participants use
an *advocacy* process, possibly the least productive way
to get things done. They view decision making as a contest, arguing passionately for their preferred solutions,
presenting information selectively, withholding relevant
conflicting data so they can make a convincing case,
and standing firm against opposition. Much more powerful is an *inquiry* process, in which people consider a

variety of options and work together to discover the best solution. Moving from advocacy to inquiry requires careful attention to three critical factors: fostering constructive, rather than personal, conflict; making sure everyone knows that their viewpoints are given serious consideration even if they are not ultimately accepted; and knowing when to bring deliberations to a close.

The authors discuss in detail strategies for moving from an advocacy to an inquiry process, as well as for fostering productive conflict, true consideration, and timely closure. And they offer a framework for assessing the effectiveness of your process while you're still in the middle of it.

Decision making is a job that lies at the very heart of leadership and one that requires a genius for balance: the ability to embrace the divergence that may characterize early discussions and to forge the unity needed for effective implementation.

LEADERS SHOW THEIR METTLE in many ways—setting strategy and motivating people, just to mention two—but above all else leaders are made or broken by the quality of their decisions. That's a given, right? If you answered yes, then you would probably be surprised by how many executives approach decision making in a way that neither puts enough options on the table nor permits sufficient evaluation to ensure that they can make the best choice. Indeed, our research over the past several years strongly suggests that, simply put, most leaders get decision making all wrong.

The reason: Most businesspeople treat decision making as an event—a discrete choice that takes place at a single point in time, whether they're sitting at a desk, moderating a meeting, or staring at a spreadsheet. This classic view of decision making has a pronouncement popping out of a leader's head, based on experience, gut, research, or all three. Say the matter at hand is whether to pull a product with weak sales off the market. An "event" leader would mull in solitude, ask for advice, read reports, mull some more, then say yea or nay and send the organization off to make it happen. But to look at decision making that way is to overlook larger social and organizational contexts, which ultimately determine the success of any decision.

The fact is, decision making is not an event. It's a process, one that unfolds over weeks, months, or even years; one that's fraught with power plays and politics and is replete with personal nuances and institutional history; one that's rife with discussion and debate; and one that requires support at all levels of the organization when it comes time for execution. Our research shows that the difference between leaders who make good decisions and those who make bad ones is striking. The former recognize that all decisions are processes, and they explicitly design and manage them as such. The latter persevere in the fantasy that decisions are events they alone control.

In the following pages, we'll explore how leaders can design and manage a sound, effective decision-making process—an approach we call inquiry—and outline a set of criteria for assessing the quality of the decision-making process. First, a look at the process itself.

Decisions as Process: Inquiry Versus Advocacy

Not all decision-making processes are equally effective, particularly in the degree to which they allow a group to identify and consider a wide range of ideas. In our research, we've seen two broad approaches. *Inquiry,* which we prefer, is a very open process designed to generate multiple alternatives, foster the exchange of ideas, and produce a well-tested solution. Unfortunately, this approach doesn't come easily or naturally to most people. Instead, groups charged with making a decision tend to default to the second mode, one we call *advocacy.* The two look deceptively similar on the surface: groups of people, immersed in discussion and debate, trying to select a course of action by drawing on what they believe is the best available evidence. But despite their similarities, inquiry and advocacy produce dramatically different results.

When a group takes an advocacy perspective, participants approach decision making as a contest, although they don't necessarily compete openly or even consciously. Well-defined groups with special interests—

Two Approaches to Decision Making

	Advocacy	Inquiry
Concept of decision making	a contest	collaborative problem solving
Purpose of discussion	persuasion and lobbying	testing and evaluation
Participants' role	spokespeople	critical thinkers
Patterns of behavior	strive to persuade others	present balanced arguments
	defend your position	remain open to alternatives
	downplay weaknesses	accept constructive criticism
Minority views	discouraged or dismissed	cultivated and valued
Outcome	winners and losers	collective ownership

dueling divisions in search of budget increases, for example—advocate for particular positions. Participants are passionate about their preferred solutions and therefore stand firm in the face of disagreement. That level of passion makes it nearly impossible to remain objective, limiting people's ability to pay attention to opposing arguments. Advocates often present information selectively, buttressing their arguments while withholding relevant conflicting data. Their goal, after all, is to make a compelling case, not to convey an evenhanded or balanced view. Two different plant managers pushing their own improvement programs, for example, may be wary of reporting potential weak points for fear that full disclosure will jeopardize their chances of winning the debate and gaining access to needed resources.

What's more, the disagreements that arise are frequently fractious and even antagonistic. Personalities and egos come into play, and differences are normally resolved through battles of wills and behind-the-scenes maneuvering. The implicit assumption is that a superior solution will emerge from a test of strength among competing positions. But in fact this approach typically suppresses innovation and encourages participants to go along with the dominant view to avoid further conflict.

By contrast, an inquiry-focused group carefully considers a variety of options and works together to discover the best solution. While people naturally continue to have their own interests, the goal is not to persuade the group to adopt a given point of view but instead to come to agreement on the best course of action. People share information widely, preferably in raw form, to allow participants to draw their own conclusions. Rather than suppressing dissension, an inquiry process encourages critical thinking. All participants feel comfortable raising alternative solutions and asking hard questions about the possibilities already on the table.

People engaged in an inquiry process rigorously question proposals and the assumptions they rest on, so conflict may be intense—but it is seldom personal. In fact, because disagreements revolve around ideas and interpretations rather than entrenched positions, conflict is generally healthy, and team members resolve their differences by applying rules of reason. The implicit assumption is that a consummate solution will emerge from a test of strength among competing ideas rather than dueling positions. Recent accounts of GE's succession process describe board members pursuing just such an open-minded approach. All members met repeatedly with the major candidates and gathered regularly to review their strengths and weaknesses—frequently without Jack Welch in attendance—with little or no attempt to lobby early for a particular choice.

A process characterized by inquiry rather than advocacy tends to produce decisions of higher quality—decisions that not only advance the company's objectives but also are reached in a timely manner and can be implemented effectively. Therefore, we believe that leaders seeking to improve their organizations' decision-making capabilities need to begin with a single goal: moving as quickly as possible from a process of advocacy to one of inquiry. That requires careful attention to three critical factors, the "three C's" of effective decision making: *conflict, consideration,* and *closure.* Each entails a delicate balancing act.

Constructive Conflict

Critical thinking and rigorous debate invariably lead to conflict. The good news is that conflict brings issues into focus, allowing leaders to make more informed choices. The bad news is that the wrong kind of conflict can derail the decision-making process altogether.

Indeed, conflict comes in two forms—*cognitive* and *affective*. Cognitive, or substantive, conflict relates to the work at hand. It involves disagreements over ideas and assumptions and differing views on the best way to proceed. Not only is such conflict healthy, it's crucial to effective inquiry. When people express differences openly and challenge underlying assumptions, they can flag real weaknesses and introduce new ideas. Affective, or interpersonal, conflict is emotional. It involves personal friction, rivalries, and clashing personalities, and it tends to diminish people's willingness to cooperate during implementation, rendering the decision-making process less effective. Not surprisingly, it is a common feature of advocacy processes.

On examination, the two are easy to distinguish. When a team member recalls "tough debates about the strategic, financial, and operating merits of the three acquisition candidates," she is referring to cognitive conflict. When a team member comments on "heated arguments that degenerated into personal attacks," he means affective conflict. But in practice the two types of conflict are surprisingly hard to separate. People tend to take any criticism personally and react defensively. The atmosphere quickly becomes charged, and even if a high quality decision emerges, the emotional fallout tends to linger, making it hard for team members to work together during implementation.

The challenge for leaders is to increase cognitive conflict while keeping affective conflict low—no mean feat. One technique is to establish norms that make vigorous debate the rule rather than the exception. Chuck Knight, for 27 years the CEO of Emerson Electric, accomplished this by relentlessly grilling managers during planning reviews, no matter what he actually thought of the proposal on the table, asking tough, combative questions and expecting well-framed responses. The process—which Knight called the "logic of illogic" because of his willingness to test even well-crafted arguments by raising unexpected, and occasionally fanciful, concerns—was undoubtedly intimidating. But during his tenure it produced a steady stream of smart investment decisions and an unbroken string of quarterly increases in net income.

Bob Galvin, when he was CEO of Motorola in the 1980s, took a slightly different approach. He habitually asked unexpected hypothetical questions that stimulated creative thinking. Subsequently, as chairman of the board of overseers for the Malcolm Baldrige National Quality Program, Galvin took his colleagues by surprise when, in response to pressure from constituents to broaden the criteria for the award, he proposed narrowing them instead. In the end, the board did in fact broaden the criteria, but his seemingly out-of-the-blue suggestion sparked a creative and highly productive debate.

Another technique is to structure the conversation so that the process, by its very nature, fosters debate. This can be done by dividing people into groups with different, and often competing, responsibilities. For example, one group may be asked to develop a proposal while the other generates alternative recommendations. Then the groups would exchange proposals and discuss the various options. Such techniques virtually guarantee high levels of cognitive conflict. (The exhibit "Structuring the Debate" outlines two approaches for using different groups to stimulate creative thinking.)

But even if you've structured the process with an eye toward encouraging cognitive conflict, there's always a risk that it will become personal. Beyond cooling the debate with "time-outs," skilled leaders use a number of

Structuring the Debate

By breaking a decision-making body into two subgroups, leaders can often create an environment in which people feel more comfortable engaging in debate. Scholars recommend two techniques in particular, which we call the "point-counterpoint" and "intellectual watchdog" approaches. The first three steps are the same for both techniques:

Point-Counterpoint	Intellectual Watchdog
The team divides into two subgroups	The team divides into two subgroups.
Subgroup A develops a proposal, fleshing out the recommendation, the key assumptions, and the critical supporting data.	Subgroup A develops a proposal, fleshing out the recommendation, the key assumptions, and the critical supporting data.
Subgroup A presents the proposal to Subgroup B in written and oral forms.	Subgroup A presents the proposal to Subgroup B in written and oral forms.
Subgroup B generates one or more alternative plans of action.	Subgroup B develops a detailed critique of these assumptions and recommendations. It presents this critique in written and oral forms. Subgroup A revises its proposal based on this feedback.
The subgroups come together to debate the proposals and seek agreement on a common set of assumptions.	The subgroups continue in this revision-critique-revision cycle until they converge on a common set of assumptions.
Based on those assumptions, the subgroups continue to debate various options and strive to agree on a common set of recommendations.	Then, the subgroups work together to develop a common set of recommendations.

creative techniques to elevate cognitive debate while minimizing affective conflict.

First, adroit leaders pay careful attention to the way issues are framed, as well as to the language used during discussions. They preface contradictory remarks or questions with phrases that remove some of the personal sting ("Your arguments make good sense, but let me play devil's advocate for a moment"). They also set ground rules about language, insisting that team members avoid words and behavior that trigger defensiveness. For instance, in the U.S. Army's after-action reviews, conducted immediately after missions to identify mistakes so they can be avoided next time, facilitators make a point of saying, "We don't use the 'b' word, and we don't use the 'f' word. We don't place blame, and we don't find fault."

Second, leaders can help people step back from their preestablished positions by breaking up natural coalitions and assigning people to tasks on some basis other than traditional loyalties. At a leading aerospace company, one business unit president had to deal with two powerful coalitions within his organization during a critical decision about entering into a strategic alliance. When he set up two groups to consider alternative alliance partners, he interspersed the groups with members of each coalition, forcing people with different interests to work with one another. He then asked both groups to evaluate the same wide range of options using different criteria (such as technological capability, manufacturing prowess, or project management skills). The two groups then shared their evaluations and worked together to select the best partner. Because nobody had complete information, they were forced to listen closely to one another.

Third, leaders can shift individuals out of well-grooved patterns, where vested interests are highest. They can, for example, ask team members to research and argue for a position they did not endorse during initial discussions. Similarly, they can assign team members to play functional or managerial roles different from their own, such as asking an operations executive to take the marketing view or asking a lower-level employee to assume the CEO's strategic perspective.

Finally, leaders can ask participants locked in debate to revisit key facts and assumptions and gather more information. Often, people become so focused on the differences between opposing positions that they reach a stalemate. Emotional conflict soon follows. Asking people to examine underlying presumptions can defuse the tension and set the team back on track. For instance, at Enron, when people disagree strongly about whether or not to apply their trading skills to a new commodity or market, senior executives quickly refocus the discussion on characteristics of industry structure and assumptions about market size and customer preferences. People quickly recognize areas of agreement, discover precisely how and why they disagree, and then focus their debate on specific issues.

Consideration

Once a decision's been made and the alternatives dismissed, some people will have to surrender the solution they preferred. At times, those who are overruled resist the outcome; at other times, they display grudging acceptance. What accounts for the difference? The critical factor appears to be the perception of fairness—what scholars call "procedural justice." The reality is that the leader will make the ultimate decision, but the people participating in the process must believe that their views were considered and that they had a genuine opportunity to influence the final decision. Researchers have found that if participants believe the process was fair, they are far more willing to commit themselves to the resulting decision even if their views did not prevail. (For a detailed discussion of this phenomenon, see W. Chan Kim and Renée Mauborgne, "Fair Process: Managing in the Knowledge Economy," HBR July–August 1997).

Many managers equate fairness with *voice*—with giving everyone a chance to express his or her own views. They doggedly work their way around the table, getting everyone's input. However, voice is not nearly as important as *consideration*—people's belief that the leader actively listened to them during the discussions and weighed their views carefully before reaching a decision. In his 1999 book, *Only the Paranoid Survive,* Intel's chairman Andy Grove describes how he explains the distinction to his middle managers: "Your criterion for involvement should be that you're heard and understood. . . . All sides cannot prevail in the debate, but all opinions have value in shaping the right answer."

In fact, voice without consideration is often damaging; it leads to resentment and frustration rather than to acceptance. When the time comes to implement the decision, people are likely to drag their feet if they sense that the decision-making process had been a sham—an exercise in going through the motions designed to validate the leader's preferred solution. This appears to have been true of the Daimler-Chrysler merger. Daimler CEO Jurgen Schrempp asked for extensive analysis and assessment of potential merger candidates but had long before settled on Chrysler as his choice. In fact, when consultants told him that his strategy was unlikely to create shareholder value, he dismissed the data and went ahead with his plans. Schrempp may have solicited views from many parties, but he clearly failed to give them much weight.

Leaders can demonstrate consideration throughout the decision-making process. At the outset, they need to convey openness to new ideas and a willingness to accept views that differ from their own. In particular, they must avoid suggesting that their minds are already made up. They should avoid disclosing their personal preferences early in the process, or they should clearly state that any initial opinions are provisional and subject to change. Or they can absent themselves from early deliberations.

During the discussions, leaders must take care to show that they are listening actively and attentively. How? By asking questions, probing for deeper explanations, echoing comments, making eye contact, and showing patience when participants explain their positions. Taking notes is an especially powerful signal, since it suggests that the leader is making a real effort to capture, understand, and evaluate people's thoughts.

And after they make the final choice, leaders should explain their logic. They must describe the rationale for their decision, detailing the criteria they used to select a course of action. Perhaps more important, they need to convey how each participant's arguments affected the final decision or explain clearly why they chose to differ with those views.

Closure

Knowing when to end deliberations is tricky; all too often decision-making bodies rush to a conclusion or else dither endlessly and decide too late. Deciding too early is as damaging as deciding too late, and both problems can usually be traced to unchecked advocacy.

DECIDING TOO EARLY

Sometimes people's desire to be considered team players overrides their willingness to engage in critical thinking and thoughtful analysis, so the group readily accepts the first remotely plausible option. Popularly known as "groupthink," this mind-set is prevalent in the presence of strong advocates, especially in new teams, whose members are still learning the rules and may be less willing to stand out as dissenters.

The danger of groupthink is not only that it suppresses the full range of options but also that unstated objections will come to the surface at some critical moment—usually at a time when aligned, cooperative action is essential to implementation. The leader of a large division of a fast-growing retailer learned this the hard way. He liked to work with a small subset of his senior team to generate options, evaluate the alternatives, and develop a plan of action, and then bring the proposal back to the full team for validation. At that point, his managers would feel they had been presented with a fait accompli and so would be reluctant to raise their concerns. As one of them put it: "Because the meeting is the wrong place to object, we don't walk out of the room as a unified group." Instead, they would reopen the debate during implementation, delaying important initiatives by many months.

As their first line of defense against groupthink, leaders need to learn to recognize latent discontent, paying special attention to body language: furrowed brows, crossed arms, or curled-up defiance. To bring disaffected people back into the discussion, it may be best to call for a break, approach dissenters one by one, encourage them to speak up, and then reconvene. GM's Alfred Sloan was famous for this approach, which he would introduce with the following speech: "I take it we are all in complete agreement on the decision here. Then I propose we postpone further discussion of the matter until our next meeting to give ourselves time to develop disagreement and perhaps gain some understanding of what the decision is all about."

Another way to avoid early closure is to cultivate minority views either through norms or through explicit rules. Minority views broaden and deepen debate; they stretch a group's thinking, even though they are seldom adopted intact. It is for this reason that Andy Grove routinely seeks input from "helpful Cassandras," people who are known for raising hard questions and offering fresh perspectives about the dangers of proposed policies.

DECIDING TOO LATE

Here, too, unchecked advocacy is frequently the source of the problem, and in these instances it takes two main forms. At times, a team hits gridlock: Warring factions refuse to yield, restating their positions over and over again. Without a mechanism for breaking the deadlock, discussions become an endless loop. At other times, people bend over backward to ensure evenhanded participation. Striving for fairness, team members insist on hearing every view and resolving every question before reaching a conclusion. This demand for certainty—for complete arguments backed by unassailable data—is its own peculiar form of advocacy. Once again, the result is usually an endless loop, replaying the same alternatives, objections, and requests for further information. Any member of the group can unilaterally derail the discussion by voicing doubts. Meanwhile, competitive pressures may be demanding an immediate response, or participants may have tuned out long ago, as the same arguments are repeated ad nauseam.

At this point, it's the leader's job to "call the question." Jamie Houghton, the longtime CEO of Corning, invented a vivid metaphor to describe this role. He spoke of wearing two hats when working with his senior team: He figuratively put on his cowboy hat when he wanted to debate with members as an equal, and he donned a bowler when, as CEO, he called the question and announced a decision. The former role allowed for challenges and continued discussion; the latter signaled an end to the debate.

The message here is that leaders—and their teams— need to become more comfortable with ambiguity and be willing to make speedy decisions in the absence of complete, unequivocal data or support. As Dean Stanley Teele of Harvard Business School was fond of telling students: "The art of management is the art of making meaningful generalizations out of inadequate facts."

A Litmus Test

Unfortunately, superior decision making is distressingly difficult to assess in real time. Successful outcomes— decisions of high quality, made in a timely manner and implemented effectively—can be evaluated only after the fact. But by the time the results are in, it's normally too late to take corrective action. Is there any way to find out earlier whether you're on the right track?

There is indeed. The trick, we believe, is to periodically assess the decision-making process, even as it is
under way. Scholars now have considerable evidence
showing that a small set of process traits is closely linked
with superior outcomes. While they are no guarantee of
success, their combined presence sharply improves the
odds that you'll make a good decision.

MULTIPLE ALTERNATIVES

When groups consider many alternatives, they engage in
more thoughtful analysis and usually avoid settling too
quickly on the easy, obvious answer. This is one reason
techniques like point-counterpoint, which requires
groups to generate at least two alternatives, are so often
associated with superior decision making. Usually, keeping track of the number of options being considered will
tell if this test has been met. But take care not to double
count. Go-no go choices involve only one option and
don't qualify as two alternatives.

ASSUMPTION TESTING

"Facts" come in two varieties: those that have been
carefully tested and those that have been merely
asserted or assumed. Effective decision-making groups
do not confuse the two. They periodically step back
from their arguments and try to confirm their assumptions by examining them critically. If they find that
some still lack hard evidence, they may elect to proceed, but they will at least know they're venturing into
uncertain territory. Alternatively, the group may desig-
nate "intellectual watchdogs" who are assigned the task

of scrutinizing the process for unchecked assumptions and challenging them on the spot.

WELL-DEFINED CRITERIA

Without crisp, clear goals, it's easy to fall into the trap of comparing apples with oranges. Competing arguments become difficult to judge, since advocates will suggest using those measures (net income, return on capital, market presence, share of mind, and so on) that favor their preferred alternative. Fuzzy thinking and long delays are the likely result.

To avoid the problem, the team should specify goals up front and revisit them repeatedly during the decision-making process. These goals can be complex and multi-faceted, quantitative and qualitative, but whatever form they take, they must remain at the fore. Studies of merger decisions have found that as the process reaches its final stages and managers feel the pressure of dead-lines and the rush to close, they often compromise or adjust the criteria they originally created for judging the appropriateness of the deal.

DISSENT AND DEBATE

David Hume, the great Scottish philosopher, argued per-suasively for the merits of debate when he observed that the "truth springs from arguments amongst friends." There are two ways to measure the health of a debate: the kinds of questions being asked and the level of listening.

Some questions open up discussion; others narrow it and end deliberations. Contrarian hypothetical questions usually trigger healthy debate. A manager who worked for former American Express CEO Harvey Golub points to a time when the company was committed to lowering credit card fees, and Golub unexpectedly proposed raising fees instead. "I don't think he meant it seriously," says the manager. "But he certainly taught us how to think about fees."

The level of listening is an equally important indicator of a healthy decision-making process. Poor listening produces flawed analysis as well as personal friction. If participants routinely interrupt one another or pile on rebuttals before digesting the preceding comment, affective conflict is likely to materialize. Civilized discussions quickly become impossible, for collegiality and group harmony usually disappear in the absence of active listening.

PERCEIVED FAIRNESS

A real-time measure of perceived fairness is the level of participation that's maintained after a key midpoint or milestone has been reached. Often, a drop in participation is an early warning of problems with implementation since some members of the group are already showing their displeasure by voting with their feet.

In fact, keeping people involved in the process is, in the end, perhaps the most crucial factor in making a decision—and making it stick. It's a job that lies at the heart of leadership and one that uniquely combines the leader's numerous talents. It requires the fortitude to promote conflict while accepting ambiguity, the wisdom to know when to bring conversations to a close, the patience to help others understand the reasoning behind your choice, and, not least, a genius for balance—the ability to embrace both the divergence that may characterize early discussions and the unity needed for effective implementation. Cyrus the Great, the founder of the Persian Empire and a renowned military leader, understood the true hallmark of leadership in the sixth century BC, when he attributed his success to "diversity in counsel, unity in command."

Advocacy Versus Inquiry in Action

The Bay of Pigs and the Cuban Missile Crisis

PERHAPS THE BEST DEMONSTRATION of advocacy versus inquiry comes from the administration of President John F. Kennedy. During his first two years in office, Kennedy wrestled with two critical foreign policy decisions: the Bay of Pigs invasion and the Cuban Missile Crisis. Both were assigned to cabinet-level task forces, involving many of the same players, the same political interests, and extremely high stakes. But the results were extraordinarily different, largely because the two groups operated in different modes.

The first group, charged with deciding whether to support an invasion of Cuba by a small army of U.S.-trained Cuban exiles, worked in advocacy mode, and the outcome is widely regarded as an example of flawed decision making. Shortly after taking office, President Kennedy learned of the planned attack on Cuba developed by the CIA during the Eisenhower administration. Backed by the Joint Chiefs of Staff, the CIA argued forcefully for the invasion and minimized the risks, filtering the information presented to the president to reinforce the agency's position. Knowledgeable individuals on the State Department's Latin America desk were excluded from deliberations because of their likely opposition.

Some members of Kennedy's staff opposed the plan but held their tongues for fear of appearing weak in the face of strong advocacy by the CIA. As a result, there was little debate, and the group failed to test some critical underlying assumptions. For example, they didn't question whether the landing would in fact lead to a rapid domestic uprising against Castro, and they failed to find out whether the exiles could fade into the mountains (which were 80 miles from the landing site) should they meet with strong resistance. The resulting invasion is generally considered to be one of the low points of the Cold War. About 100 lives were lost, and the rest of the exiles were taken hostage. The incident was a major embarrassment to the Kennedy administration and dealt a blow to America's global standing.

After the botched invasion, Kennedy conducted a review of the foreign policy decision-making process and introduced five major changes, essentially transforming the process into one of inquiry. First, people were urged to participate in discussions as "skeptical generalists"— that is, as disinterested critical thinkers rather than as representatives of particular departments. Second, Robert Kennedy and Theodore Sorensen were assigned the role of intellectual watchdog, expected to pursue every possible point of contention, uncovering weaknesses and untested assumptions. Third, task forces were urged to abandon the rules of protocol, eliminating formal agendas and deference to rank. Fourth, participants were expected to split occasionally into subgroups to develop a broad range of options. And finally, President Kennedy decided to absent himself from some of the early task force meetings to avoid influencing other participants and slanting the debate.

The inquiry mode was used to great effect when in October 1962 President Kennedy learned that the Soviet Union had placed nuclear missiles on Cuban soil, despite repeated assurances from the Soviet ambassador that this would not occur. Kennedy immediately convened a high-level task force, which contained many of the same men responsible for the Bay of Pigs invasion, and asked them to frame a response. The group met night and day for two weeks, often inviting additional members to join in their deliberations to broaden their perspective. Occasionally, to encourage the free flow of ideas, they met without the president. Robert Kennedy played his new role thoughtfully, critiquing options frequently and encouraging the group to develop additional alternatives. In particular, he urged the group to move beyond a simple go-no-go decision on a military air strike.

Ultimately, subgroups developed two positions, one favoring a blockade and the other an air strike. These groups gathered information from a broad range of sources, viewed and interpreted the same intelligence photos, and took great care to identify and test underlying assumptions, such as whether the Tactical Air Command was indeed capable of eliminating all Soviet missiles in a surgical air strike. The subgroups exchanged position papers, critiqued each other's proposals, and came together to debate the alternatives. They presented Kennedy with both options, leaving him to make the final choice. The result was a carefully framed response, leading to a successful blockade and a peaceful end to the crisis.

Originally published in September 2001
Reprint R0108G

Change Through Persuasion

DAVID A. GARVIN AND

MICHAEL A. ROBERTO

Executive Summary

FACED WITH THE NEED for a massive change, most managers respond predictably. They revamp the organization's strategy, shift around staff, and root out inefficiencies. They then wait patiently for performance to improve—only to be bitterly disappointed because they've failed to adequately prepare employees for the change. In this article, the authors contend that to make change stick, leaders must conduct an effective persuasion campaign—one that begins weeks or months before the turnaround plan is set in concrete.

Like a political campaign, a persuasion campaign is largely one of differentiation from the past. Turnaround leaders must convince people that the organization is truly on its deathbed—or, at the very least, that radical changes are required if the organization is to survive and thrive. (This is a particularly difficult challenge when years of persistent problems have been accompanied by few changes in the status quo.) And they must demonstrate through word and deed that they are the right leaders with the right plan.

Accomplishing all this calls for a four-part communications strategy. Prior to announcing a turnaround plan, leaders need to set the stage for employees' acceptance of it. At the time of delivery, they must present a framework through which employees can interpret information and messages about the plan. As time passes, they must manage the mood so that employees' emotional states support implementation and follow-through. And at critical intervals, they must provide reinforcement to ensure that the desired changes take hold and that there's no backsliding.

Using the example of the dramatic turnaround at Boston's Beth Israel Deaconess Medical Center, the authors elucidate the inner workings of a successful change effort.

Faced with the need for massive change, most managers respond predictably. They revamp the organization's strategy, then round up the usual set of suspects—people, pay, and processes—shifting around staff, realigning incentives, and rooting out inefficiencies. They then wait patiently for performance to improve, only to be bitterly disappointed. For some reason, the right things still don't happen.

Why is change so hard? First of all, most people are reluctant to alter their habits. What worked in the past is good enough; in the absence of a dire threat, employees will keep doing what they've always done. And when an organization has had a succession of leaders, resistance to change is even stronger. A legacy of disappointment and distrust creates an environment in which employees automatically condemn the next turnaround champion to failure, assuming that he or she is "just like all the others." Calls for sacrifice and self-discipline are met with cynicism, skepticism, and knee-jerk resistance.

Our research into organizational transformation has involved settings as diverse as multinational corporations, government agencies, nonprofits, and high-performing teams like mountaineering expeditions and firefighting crews. We've found that for change to stick, leaders must design and run an effective persuasion campaign—one that begins weeks or months before the actual turnaround plan is set in concrete. Managers must perform significant work up front to ensure that employees will actually listen to tough messages, question old assumptions, and consider new ways of working. This means taking a series of deliberate but subtle steps to recast employees' prevailing views and create a new context for action. Such a shaping process must be actively managed during the first few months of a turnaround, when uncertainty is high and setbacks are inevitable. Otherwise, there is little hope for sustained improvement.

Like a political campaign, a persuasion campaign is largely one of differentiation from the past. To the typical change-averse employee, all restructuring plans look alike. The trick for turnaround leaders is to show employees precisely how their plans differ from their predecessors'. They must convince people that the organization is truly on its deathbed—or, at the very least, that radical changes are required if it is to survive and thrive. (This is a particularly difficult challenge when years of persistent problems have been accompanied by few changes in the status quo.) Turnaround leaders must also gain trust by demonstrating through word and deed that they are the right leaders for the job and must convince employees that theirs is the correct plan for moving forward.

Accomplishing all this calls for a four-part communications strategy. Prior to announcing a policy or issuing a set of instructions, leaders need to set the stage for acceptance. At the time of delivery, they must create the frame through which information and messages are interpreted. As time passes, they must manage the mood so that employees' emotional states support implementation and follow-through. And at critical intervals, they must provide reinforcement to ensure that the desired changes take hold without backsliding. See the exhibit "The Four Phases of a Persuasion Campaign" for a graphical reproduction.

In this article, we describe this process in more detail, drawing on the example of the turnaround of Beth Israel Deaconess Medical Center (BIDMC) in Boston. Paul Levy, who became CEO in early 2002, managed to bring the failing hospital back from the brink of ruin. We had ringside seats during the first six months of the turnaround. Levy agreed to hold videotaped interviews with us every two to four weeks during that period as we prepared a case study describing his efforts. He also gave us access to his daily calendar, as well as to assorted e-mail correspondence and internal memorandums and reports. From this wealth of data, we were able to track the change process as it unfolded, without the usual biases and distortions that come from 20/20 hindsight. The story of how Levy tilled the soil for change provides lessons for any CEO in a turnaround situation.

The Four Phases of a Persuasion Campaign

A typical turnaround process consists of two stark phases: plan development, followed by an implementation that may or may not be welcomed by the organization. For the turnaround plan to be widely accepted and adopted, however, the CEO must develop a separate persuasion campaign, the goal of which is to create a continuously receptive environment for change. The campaign begins well before the CEO's first day on the job—or, if the CEO is long established, well before formal development work begins—and continues long after the final plan is announced.

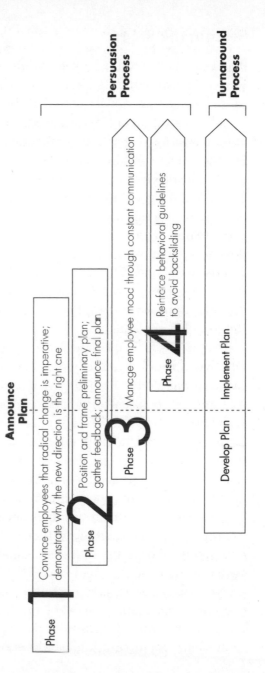

Announce Plan

Phase 1 Convince employees that radical change is imperative; demonstrate why the new direction is the right one

Phase 2 Position and frame preliminary plan; gather feedback; announce final plan

Phase 3 Manage employee mood through constant communication

Phase 4 Reinforce behavioral guidelines to avoid backsliding

Persuasion Process

Turnaround Process

Develop Plan   Implement Plan

Setting the Stage

Paul Levy was an unlikely candidate to run BIDMC. He was not a doctor and had never managed a hospital, though he had previously served as the executive dean for administration at Harvard Medical School. His claim to fame was his role as the architect of the Boston Harbor Cleanup, a multibillion-dollar pollution-control project that he had led several years earlier. (Based on this experience, Levy identified a common yet insidiously destructive organizational dynamic that causes dedicated teams to operate in counterproductive ways, which he described in "The Nut Island Effect: When Good Teams Go Wrong," HBR March 2001.) Six years after completing the Boston Harbor project, Levy approached the BIDMC board and applied for the job of cleaning up the troubled hospital.

Despite his lack of hospital management experience, Levy was appealing to the board. The Boston Harbor Cleanup was a difficult, highly visible change effort that required deft political and managerial skills. Levy had stood firm in the face of tough negotiations and often-heated public resistance and had instilled accountability in city and state agencies. He was also a known quantity to the board, having served on a BIDMC steering committee formed by the board chairman in 2001.

Levy saw the prospective job as one of public service. BIDMC was the product of a difficult 1996 merger between two hospitals—Beth Israel and Deaconess— each of which had distinguished reputations, several best-in-the-world departments and specializations, and deeply devoted staffs. The problems began after the merger. A misguided focus on clinical practice rather than backroom integration, a failure to cut costs, and the repeated inability to execute plans and adapt to changing conditions in the health-care marketplace all contributed to BIDMC's dismal performance.

By the time the board settled on Levy, affairs at BIDMC had reached the nadir. The hospital was losing $50 million a year. Relations between the administration and medical staff were strained, as were those between management and the board of directors. Employees felt demoralized, having witnessed the rapid decline in their institution's once-legendary status and the disappointing failure of its past leaders. A critical study was conducted by the Hunter Group, a leading health care consulting firm. The report, detailing the dire conditions at the hospital and the changes needed to turn things around, had been completed but not yet released. Meanwhile, the state attorney general, who was responsible for overseeing charitable trusts, had put pressure on the board to sell the failing BIDMC to a for-profit institution.

Like many CEOs recruited to fix a difficult situation, Levy's first task was to gain a mandate for the changes ahead. He also recognized that crucial negotiations were best conducted before he took the job, when his leverage was greatest, rather than after taking the reins. In particular, he moved to secure the cooperation of the hospital board by flatly stating his conditions for employment. He told the directors, for example, that should they hire him, they could no longer interfere in day-to-day management decisions. In his second and third meetings with the board's search committee, Levy laid out his timetable and intentions. He insisted that the board decide on his appointment quickly so that he could be on the job before the release of the Hunter report. He told the committee that he intended to push for a smaller, more effective group of directors. Though the conditions were somewhat unusual, the board was convinced that Levy had the experience to lead a successful turnaround, and they accepted his terms. Levy went to work on January 7, 2002.

The next task was to set the stage with the hospital staff. Levy was convinced that the employees, hungry for a turnaround, would do their best to cooperate with him if he could emulate and embody the core values of the hospital culture, rather than impose his personal values. He chose to act as the managerial equivalent of a good doctor—that is, as one who, in dealing with a very ill patient, delivers both the bad news and the chances of success honestly and imparts a realistic sense of hope, without sugar coating.

Like any leader facing a turnaround, Levy also knew he had to develop a bold message that provided compelling reasons to do things differently and then cast that message in capital letters to signal the arrival of a new order. To give his message teeth, he linked it to an implicit threat. Taking his cue from his private discussions with the state attorney general, whom he had persuaded to keep the hospital open for the time being, Levy chose to publicize the very real possibility the hospital would be sold. While he realized he risked frightening the staff and the patients with this bad news, he believed that a strong wake-up call was necessary to get employees to face up to the situation.

During his first morning on the job, Levy delivered an all-hands-on-deck e-mail to the staff. The memo contained four broad messages. It opened with the good news, pointing out that the organization had much to be proud of ("This is a wonderful institution, representing the very best in academic medicine: exemplary patient care, extraordinary research, and fine

teaching"). Second, Levy noted that the threat of sale
was real ("This is our last chance"). Third, he signaled
the kinds of actions employees could expect him to
take ("There will be a reduction in staff"). And finally,
he described the open management style he would
adopt. He would manage by walking around—lunching
with staff in the cafeteria, having impromptu conversations in the hallways, talking with employees at every
opportunity to discover their concerns. He would communicate directly with employees through e-mail rather
than through intermediaries. He also noted that the
Hunter report would be posted on the hospital intranet,
where all employees would have the opportunity to review its recommendations and submit comments for
the final turnaround plan. The direct, open tone of the
e-mail memo signaled exactly how Levy's management
style would differ from that of his predecessors.

In the afternoon, he disclosed BIDMC's situation
in interviews with the *Boston Globe* and the *Boston
Herald,* the city's two major newspapers. He told
reporters the same thing he had told the hospital's
employees: that, in the absence of a turnaround, the
hospital would be sold to a for-profit chain and would
therefore lose its status as a Harvard teaching hospital.
Staving off a sale would require tough measures,
including the laying off of anywhere from 500 to 700
employees. Levy insisted that there would be no nursing layoffs, in keeping with the hospital's core values
of high-quality patient care. The newspaper reports,
together with the memo circulated that morning,
served to immediately reset employee expectations
while dramatically increasing staff cooperation and
willingness to accept whatever new initiatives might
prove necessary to the hospital's survival.

Two days later, the critical Hunter report came out and was circulated via the hospital's intranet. Because the report had been produced by an objective third party, employees were open to its unvarnished, warts-and-all view of the hospital's current predicament. The facts were stark, and the staff could no longer claim ignorance. Levy received, and personally responded to, more than 300 e-mail suggestions for improvement in response to the report, many of which he later included in the turnaround plan.

Creating the Frame

Once the stage has been set for acceptance, effective leaders need to help employees interpret proposals for change. Complex plans can be interpreted in any number of ways; not all of them ensure acceptance and favorable outcomes. Skilled leaders therefore use "frames" to provide context and shape perspective for new proposals and plans. By framing the issues, leaders help people digest ideas in particular ways. A frame can take many forms: It can be a companywide presentation that prepares employees before an unexpected change, for example, or a radio interview that provides context following an unsettling layoff.

Levy used one particularly effective framing device to help employees interpret a preliminary draft of the turnaround plan. This device took the form of a detailed e-mail memo accompanying the dense, several-hundred-page plan. The memo explained, in considerable detail, the plan's purpose and expected impact.

The first section of the memo sought to mollify critics and reduce the fears of doctors and nurses. Its tone was positive and uplifting; it discussed BIDMC's mission, strategy, and uncompromising values, emphasizing the hospital's "warm, caring environment." This section of the letter also reaffirmed the importance of remaining an academic medical center, as well as reminding employees of their shared mission and ideals. The second part of the letter told employees what to expect, providing further details about the turnaround plan. It emphasized that tough measures and goals would be required but noted that the specific recommendations were based, for the most part, on the advice in the Hunter report, which employees had already reviewed. The message to employees was, "You've already seen and endorsed the Hunter report. There are no future surprises."

The third part of the letter anticipated and responded to prospective concerns; this had the effect of circumventing objections. This section explicitly diagnosed past plans and explained their deficiencies, which were largely due to their having been imposed top-down, with little employee ownership, buy-in, or discussion. Levy then offered a direct interpretation of what had gone wrong. Past plans, he said, had underestimated the size of the financial problem, set unrealistic expectations for new revenue growth, and failed to test implementation proposals. This section of the letter also drove home the need for change at a deeper, more visceral level than employees had experienced in the past. It emphasized that this plan was a far more collective effort than past proposals had been, because it incorporated many employee suggestions.

By framing the turnaround proposal this way, Levy accomplished two things. First, he was able to convince employees that the plan belonged to them. Second, the letter served as the basis for an ongoing communication platform. Levy reiterated its points at every opportunity—not only with employees but also in public meetings and in discussions with the press.

Managing the Mood

Turnarounds are depressing events, especially when they involve restructuring and downsizing. Relationships are disrupted, friends move on, and jobs disappear. In such settings, managing the mood of the organization becomes an essential leadership skill. Leaders must pay close attention to employees' emotions—the ebb and flow of their feelings and moods—and work hard to preserve a receptive climate for change. Often, this requires a delicate balancing act between presenting good and bad news in just the right proportion. Employees need to feel that their sacrifices have not been in vain and that their accomplishments have been recognized and rewarded. At the same time, they must be reminded that complacency is not an option. The communication challenge is daunting. One must strike the right notes of optimism and realism and carefully calibrate the timing, tone, and positioning of every message.

Paul Levy's challenge was threefold: to give remaining employees time to grieve and recover from layoffs and other difficult measures; to make them feel that he cared for and supported them; and to ensure that the turnaround plan proceeded apace. The process depended on mutual trust and employees' desire to succeed. "I had to calibrate the push and pull of congratulations and pressure, but I also depended on the staff's underlying value system and sense of mission," he said. "They were highly motivated, caring individuals who had stuck with the place through five years of hell. They wanted to do good."

The first step was to acknowledge employees' feelings of depression while helping them look to the future. Immediately after the first round of layoffs, people were feeling listless and dejected; Levy knew that releasing the final version of the turnaround plan too soon after the layoffs could be seen as cold. In an e-mail he sent to all employees a few days later, Levy explicitly empathized with employees' feelings ("This week is a sad one . . . it is hard for those of us remaining . . . offices are emptier than usual"). He then urged employees to look forward and concluded on a strongly optimistic note (". . . our target is not just survival: It is to thrive and set an example for what a unique academic medical center like ours means for this region"). His upbeat words were reinforced by a piece of good luck that weekend when the underdog New England Patriots won their first Super Bowl championship in dramatic fashion in the last 90 seconds of the game. When Levy returned to work the following Monday, employees were saying, "If the Patriots can do it, we can, too."

The next task was to keep employees focused on the continuing hard work ahead. On April 12, two months into the restructuring process, Levy sent out a "Frequently Asked Questions" e-mail giving a generally favorable view of progress to date. At the same time, he spoke plainly about the need to control costs and reminded employees that merit pay increases would remain on hold. This was hardly the rosy picture that most employees were hoping for, of course. But Levy believed sufficient time had passed that employees could accommodate a more realistic and tough tone on his part.

A month later, everything changed. Operational improvements that were put in place during the first phase of the turnaround had begun to take hold. Financial performance was well ahead of budget, with the best results since the merger. In another e-mail, Levy praised employees lavishly. He also convened a series of open question-and-answer forums, where employees heard more details about the hospital's tangible progress and received kudos for their accomplishments.

Reinforcing Good Habits

Without a doubt, the toughest challenge faced by leaders during a turnaround is to avoid backsliding into dysfunctional routines—habitual patterns of negative behavior by individuals and groups that are triggered automatically and unconsciously by familiar circumstances or stimuli. (For more on how such disruptive patterns work, see "Dysfunctional Routines: Six Ways to Stop Change in Its Tracks" at the end of this article.) Employees need help maintaining new behaviors, especially when their old ways of working are deeply ingrained and destructive. Effective change leaders provide opportunities for employees to practice desired behaviors repeatedly, while personally modeling new ways of working and providing coaching and support.

In our studies of successful turnarounds, we've found that effective leaders explicitly reinforce organizational values on a constant basis, using actions to back up their words. Their goal is to change behavior, not just ways of thinking. For example, a leader can talk about values such as openness, tolerance, civility, teamwork, delegation, and direct communication in meetings and e-mails.

But the message takes hold only if he or she also signals a dislike of disruptive, divisive behaviors by pointedly—and, if necessary, publicly—criticizing them.

At Beth Israel Deaconess Medical Center, the chiefs of medicine, surgery, orthopedics, and other key functions presented Levy with special behavioral challenges, particularly because he was not a doctor. Each medical chief was in essence a "mini-dean," the head of a largely self-contained department with its own faculty, staff, and resources. As academic researchers, they were rewarded primarily for individual achievement. They had limited experience solving business or management problems.

In dealing with the chiefs, Levy chose an approach that blended with a strong dose of discipline with real-time, public reinforcement. He developed guidelines for behavior and insisted that everyone in the hospital measure up to them. In one of his earliest meetings with the chiefs, Levy presented a simple set of "meeting rules," including such chestnuts as "state your objections" and "disagree without being disagreeable," and led a discussion about them, demonstrating the desired behaviors through his own leadership of the meeting. The purpose of these rules was to introduce new standards of interpersonal behavior and, in the process, to combat several dysfunctional routines.

One serious test of Levy's ability to reinforce these norms came a month and a half after he was named CEO. After a staff meeting at which all the department chairs were present, one chief—who had remained silent—sent an e-mail to Levy complaining about a decision made during the meeting. The e-mail copied the other chiefs as well as the chairman of the board. Many CEOs would choose to criticize such behavior privately.

But Levy responded in an e-mail to the same audience, publicly denouncing the chief for his tone, his lack of civility, and his failure to speak up earlier in the process, as required by the new meeting rules. It was as close to a public hanging as anyone could get. Several of the chiefs privately expressed their support to Levy; they too had been offended by their peer's presumptuousness. More broadly, the open criticism served to powerfully reinforce new norms while curbing disruptive behavior.

Even as they must set expectations and reinforce behaviors, effective change leaders also recognize that many employees simply do not know how to make decisions as a group or work cooperatively. By delegating critical decisions and responsibilities, a leader can provide employees with ample opportunities to practice new ways of working; in such cases, employees' performance should be evaluated as much on their adherence to the new standards and processes as on their substantive choices. In this spirit, Levy chose to think of himself primarily as a kind of appeals court judge. When employees came to him seeking his intervention on an issue or situation, he explained, he would "review the process used by the 'lower court' to determine if it followed the rules. If so, the decision stands." He did not review cases de novo and substitute his judgment for that of the individual department or unit. He insisted that employees work through difficult issues themselves, even when they were not so inclined, rather than rely on him to tell them what to do. At other times, he intervened personally and coached employees when they lacked basic skills. When two members of his staff disagreed on a proposed course of action, Levy triggered an open, emotional debate, then worked with the participants and their bosses behind the scenes to resolve the differences. At the next staff meeting, he praised the participants' willingness to disagree publicly, reemphasizing that vigorous debate was healthy and desirable and that confrontation was not to be avoided. In this way, employees gained experience in working through their problems on their own.

Performance, of course, is the ultimate measure of a successful turnaround. On that score, BIDMC has done exceedingly well since Levy took the helm. The original restructuring plan called for a three-year improvement process, moving from a $58 million loss in 2001 to breakeven in 2004. At the end of the 2004 fiscal year, performance was far ahead of plan, with the hospital reporting a $37.4 million net gain from operations. Revenues were up, while costs were sharply reduced. Decision making was now crisper and more responsive, even though there was little change in the hospital's senior staff or medical leadership. Morale, not surprisingly, was up as well. To take just one indicator, annual nursing turnover, which was 15% to 16% when Levy became CEO, had dropped to 3% by mid-2004. Pleased with the hospital's performance, the board signed Levy to a new three-year contract.

Heads, Hearts, and Hands

It's clear that the key to Paul Levy's success at Beth Israel Deaconess Medical Center is that he understood the importance of making sure the cultural soil had been made ready before planting the seeds of change. In a receptive environment, employees not only understand why change is necessary; they're also emotionally committed to making it happen, and they faithfully execute the required steps.

On a cognitive level, employees in receptive environments are better able to let go of competing, unsubstantiated views of the nature and extent of the problems facing their organizations. They hold the same, objective views of the causes of poor performance. They acknowledge the seriousness of current financial, operational, and marketplace difficulties. And they take responsibility for their own contributions to those problems. Such a shared, fact-based diagnosis is crucial for moving forward.

On an emotional level, employees in receptive environments identify with the organization and its values and are committed to its continued existence. They believe that the organization stands for something more than profitability, market share, or stock performance and is therefore worth saving. Equally important, they trust the leader, believing that he or she shares their values and will fight to preserve them. Leaders earn considerable latitude from employees—and their proposals usually get the benefit of the doubt—when their hearts are thought to be in the right place.

Workers in such environments also have physical, hands-on experience with the new behaviors expected of them. They have seen the coming changes up close and understand what they are getting into. In such an atmosphere where it's acceptable for employees to wrestle with decisions on their own and practice unfamiliar ways of working, a leader can successfully allay irrational fears and undercut the myths that so often accompany major change efforts.

There is a powerful lesson in all this for leaders. To create a receptive environment, persuasion is the ultimate tool. Persuasion promotes understanding; understanding breeds acceptance; acceptance leads to action. Without persuasion, even the best of turnaround plans will fail to take root.

Dysfunctional Routines: Six Ways to Stop Change in Its Tracks

JUST AS PEOPLE ARE CREATURES of habit, organizations thrive on routines. Management teams, for example, routinely cut budgets after performance deviates from plan. Routines—predictable, virtually automatic behaviors—are unstated, self-reinforcing, and remarkably resilient. Because they lead to more efficient cognitive processing, they are, for the most part, functional and highly desirable.

Dysfunctional routines, by contrast, are barriers to action and change. Some are outdated behaviors that were appropriate once but are now unhelpful. Others manifest themselves in knee-jerk reactions, passivity, unproductive foot-dragging, and, sometimes, active resistance.

Dysfunctional routines are persistent, but they are not unchangeable. Novelty—the perception that current circumstances are truly different from those that previously prevailed—is one of the most potent forces for dislodging routines. To overcome them, leaders must clearly signal that the context has changed. They must work directly with employees to recognize and publicly examine dysfunctional routines and substitute desired behaviors.

A culture of "no."

In organizations dominated by cynics and critics, there is always a good reason not to do something. Piling on criticism is an easy way to avoid taking risks and claim false superiority. Lou Gerstner gets credit for naming this routine, which he found on his arrival at IBM, but it is common in many organizations. Another CEO described her team's response to new initiatives by likening it to a skeet shoot. "Someone would yell, 'Pull!', there would be a deafening blast, and the idea would be in pieces on the ground." This routine has two sources: a culture that overvalues criticism and analysis, and complex decision-making processes requiring multiple approvals, in which anybody can say "no" but nobody can say "yes." It is especially likely in organizations that are divided into large subunits or segments, led by local leaders with great power who are often unwilling to comply with directives from above.

The dog and pony show must go on.

Some organizations put so much weight on process that they confuse ends and means, form and content. How you present a proposal becomes more important than what you propose. Managers construct presentations carefully and devote large amounts of time to obtaining sign-offs. The result is death by PowerPoint. Despite the appearance of progress, there's little real headway.

The grass is always greener.

To avoid facing challenges in their core business, some managers look to new products, new services, and new lines of business. At times, such diversification is healthy. But all too often these efforts are merely an avoidance tactic that keeps tough problems at arm's length.

After the meeting ends, debate begins.

This routine is often hard to spot because so much of it takes place under cover. Cordial, apparently coopera-tive meetings are followed by resistance. Sometimes, resisters are covert; often, they end-run established forums entirely and take their concerns directly to the top. The result? Politics triumphs over substance, staff meetings become empty rituals, and meddling becomes the norm.

Ready, aim, aim . . .

Here, the problem is the organization's inability to settle on a definitive course of action. Staff members generate a continual stream of proposals and reports; managers repeatedly tinker with each one, fine-tuning their choices without ever making a final decision. Often called "analysis paralysis," this pattern is common in perfectionist cultures where mistakes are career threatening and people who rock the boat drown.

This too shall pass.

In organizations where prior leaders repeatedly proclaimed a state of crisis but then made few substantive changes, employees tend to be jaded. In such situations, they develop a heads-down, bunker mentality and a reluctance to respond to management directives. Most believe that the wisest course of action is to ignore new initiatives, work around them, or wait things out.

Originally published in February 2005
Reprint R0502F

About the Contributors

L.M. BAKER, JR. was chairman of Wachovia in Charlotte, North Carolina, until his retirement in 2003.

ROBERT D. BALLARD, whose team discovered the *Titanic*, the *Bismarck*, and *PT-109*, is the president of the Institute for Exploration in Mystic, Connecticut, and director of the University of Rhode Island's Institute for Underwater Archaeology at its Graduate School of Oceanography.

CHRISTOPHER BANGLE is global chief of design at BMW in Munich, Germany.

HERB BAUM is chairman, president, and CEO of the Dial Corporation in Scottsdale, Arizona.

SUSAN BUTCHER was a four-time winner of the 1,150-mile Iditarod sled dog race.

LIU CHUANZHI is chairman of Lenovo Group.

ROBERT B. CIALDINI is the Regents' Professor of Psychology at Arizona State University and the author of *Influence: Science and Practice* (Allyn & Bacon, 2001).

JAY A. CONGER is the Henry R. Kravis Research Chair in Leadership Studies at Claremont-McKenna College in California.

ROBERT A. ECKERT is chairman and CEO of Mattel in El Segundo, California.

CARLY FIORINA was chairman and CEO of Hewlett-Packard in Palo Alto, California, from 1999 to 2005.

DAVID A. GARVIN is the C. Roland Christensen Professor of Business Administration at Harvard Business School in Boston.

MICHAEL MACCOBY is the founder and president of the Maccoby Group, a management consultancy in Washington, DC.

MARIO MAZZOLA is the chief development officer at Cisco Systems in San Jose, California.

HANK MCKINNELL was the chairman and CEO of Pfizer in New York from 2001 to 2006.

DEBRA E. MEYERSON is the author of *Tempered Radicals: How People Use Differences to Inspire Change at Work* (Harvard Business School Press, 2001). She is Associate Professor of Organizational Behavior at Stanford University's School of Education and (by courtesy) Graduate School of Business, and codirector of Stanford's Center for Research in Philanthropy and Civil Society.

ROBERT B. MILLER is the chairman of Miller-Williams Incorporated, a San Diego-based customer research firm.

ROSS J. PILLARI is the president of BP America in Warrenville, Illinois, and is a group vice president of London-based BP PLC.

MICHAEL A. ROBERTO is an assistant professor of business administration at Harvard Business School in Boston.

CHAUNCEY VEATCH works at Coachella Valley High School in Thermal, California, and was 2002 National Teacher of the Year.

GARY A. WILLIAMS is the CEO of Miller-Williams Incorporated, a San Diego-based customer research firm.

Index

"intellectual watchdog" approach, 153, 161–162, 165
irrational motivations. *See* emotions; transference

Jason Project, Galápagos Islands, 63–64
Jobs, Steve, 141
Johnson, Lyndon, 138
Jordan, Michael, 140–141
Journal of Abnormal and Social Psychology, 39
Journal of Applied Psychology, 36, 44
Journal of Consumer Research, 32
Journal of Experimental Social Psychology, 33
Journal of Personality and Social Psychology, 36–37

Kelleher, Herb, 72, 74
Kennedy, John F. (U.S. president), 164–166
Kennedy, Robert, 165
key people
    emotional connection and, 20, 22–23
    endorsements by, 83
    information exclusivity and, 44–45
    preliminary conversations with, 9, 10, 16, 76
    strategic alliance building and, 96, 98, 110–113

strategic alliances and, 110–113
Kim, W. Chan, 156
Knight, Chuck, 151–152
Knishinsky, Amram, 44

language, power of, 2, 16–19
Lansing, Sherry, 133
leader-follower relationships. *See* transference
leaders, transference by, 127–128
learning, 55–56. *See also* preparation
Legend Group, Beijing, 64–65
Levy, Paul, 170, 172–184. *See also* persuasion campaign
line employees. *See* staff and line employees
Linnett, Barry, 11–13, 17–18
listening
    consideration and, 157
    framing and, 15–16
    level of, and debate, 162, 163
    radical change and, 106–107
"logic of illogic," 152
"loss language," 44
loyalty
    natural coalitions and, 154
    transference and, 131–132

Malcolm Baldrige National Quality Program, 152
"management by consequence," 140
manipulation, 3, 46–47